CB

CBT for Career Success is a unique self-help book, offering a powerful combination of cognitive and behavioural therapy (CBT) approaches alongside career coaching for the first time. Whether you are just starting out in your career, aiming at a more senior position or considering a change in direction, this book is for you.

If you want to succeed in the labour market, you need a psychological edge to help you progress in an increasingly competitive and volatile job market. This book provides powerful CBT approaches that will strengthen your resilience and motivation and increase the sheer excitement and enjoyment of achieving success in the workplace. The book provides clear, practical strategies and a wealth of materials that will help you to define your personal values and match them with suitable career choices, use psychological and motivational techniques to succeed in a competitive environment and deal effectively with work related stress.

The materials included within this book have been used on training courses delivered to hundreds of career counsellors and coaches in different parts of England in recent years and have helped them to support their clients more effectively.

CBT for Career Success will be of interest to all those wishing to succeed in their chosen careers, including new entrants to the labour market.

Steve Sheward is a Career Counsellor and Senior CBT Therapist in the National Health Service. He has used his experience of working in both professions to develop a unique combination of CBT with career counselling and coaching. He has worked as a senior manager within the national career service in the UK and delivers CBT based career counselling courses throughout England.

Aberdeenshire

3188343

CBT for Career Success

A self-help guide

Steve Sheward

Routledge
Taylor & Francis Group

LONDON AND NEW YORK

First published 2016
by Routledge
2 Park Square, Milton Park, Abingdon, Oxon OX14 4RN

and by Routledge
711 Third Avenue, New York, NY 10017

Routledge is an imprint of the Taylor & Francis Group, an informa business

British Library Cataloguing in Publication Data
A catalogue record for this book is available from the British Library

Library of Congress Cataloging in Publication Data
Names: Sheward, Steve, author.
Title: CBT for career success : a self-help guide / Steve Sheward.
Other titles: Cognitive behavior therapy for career success
Description: New York : Routledge, 2016.
Identifiers: LCCN 2015040439 (print) | LCCN 2016011357 (ebook)
| ISBN 9781138838000 (hardback) | ISBN 9781138838017 (pbk.) |
ISBN 9781315728414 (ebook)
Subjects: LCSH: Career development. | Vocational guidance—Psychological
aspects. | Job stress. | Cognitive therapy.
Classification: LCC HF5381 .S5478 2016 (print) | LCC HF5381 (ebook) |
DDC 650.1—dc23
LC record available at http://lccn.loc.gov/2015040439

ISBN: 978-1-138-83800-0 (hbk)
ISBN: 978-1-138-83801-7 (pbk)
ISBN: 978-1-315-72841-4 (ebk)

Typeset in Times New Roman
by diacriTech, Chennai
Printed in Great Britain by
Ashford Colour Press Ltd, Gosport, Hants

MIX
Paper from
responsible sources
FSC® C011748

This book is dedicated to my mother and father and my wife Stella

About the author

Steve Sheward is qualified as both a career counsellor and cognitive behavioural therapist and has used his experience of working in both professions to develop a unique combination of cognitive behavioural approaches with career counselling and coaching. Steve is accredited with the BABCP, AREBT and BACP. He has worked as a senior manager within the UK career service for over 10 years, was director of the Connexions Service in South London and also managed a range of national adult career counselling services including projects targeting support at unemployed clients. Steve currently works in London for the National Health Service as a senior CBT therapist, where he treats patients for a range of psychological problems including depression, anxiety, obsessive compulsive disorder and post-traumatic stress disorder. Steve also supervises the work of other clinicians within the NHS and has delivered numerous training courses throughout England combining cognitive behavioural approaches with the use of career counselling and coaching to motivate clients. Steve practises karate and holds a second dan black belt.

Previously published work

Motivational Career Counselling and Coaching: Cognitive and Behavioural Approaches with Rhena Branch as second author
SAGE 2012

Contents

Introduction

CBT for Career Success is unique. It's the first self-help book to combine powerful cognitive and behavioural approaches with motivational career coaching techniques, and it will give you a competitive edge.

Chapter 1 will provide you with a detailed introduction to the theory and practice of cognitive and behavioural approaches and how you can utilise them to achieve your career goals. You'll learn how your thoughts, emotions, physiology and behaviours interact in complex ways and how your perception is influenced by challenging situations such as job interviews or working in a high pressure environment. I'll teach you how to spot unhelpful thinking patterns and I'll provide you with strategies to counter self-limiting beliefs. You'll become an expert in carrying out formulations of how you think, feel and act in challenging situations so that you can develop a confident frame of mind and act accordingly. You will also obtain detailed knowledge of the way emotions work and how to harness these powerful drives.

After you've gained an understanding of cognitive and behavioural theory, I'll introduce you to a range of motivational techniques in Chapter 2 that will help you to achieve success at interview. You will learn to manage anxiety, focus your attention under pressure and maximise motivation. I'll teach you how to enter into a supreme state of confidence by using a combination of relaxation and visualisation techniques. I'll also provide you with advice on getting a good night's sleep before the interview or any other potentially stressful event.

One of the most important decisions you will make in life is choosing your next career direction. In Chapter 3, I'll provide you with various methods for making effective career choices, including building a compelling vision for the future, goal setting and maintaining motivation in the face of setbacks. I'll help you to identify your personal values and show you how they can guide you like an inner compass when making important career decisions. You'll learn about the concept of *flow* and how to obtain profound job satisfaction. You will also gain insight into your personal psychological barriers to success and I'll teach you how to break through your comfort zone to achieve your ambitions.

Chapter 4 will provide you with a range of cognitive and behavioural strategies to help you achieve success in the workplace. I'll teach you stress-busting techniques and how to increase your tolerance of uncertainty in an uncertain world. You'll learn how to become super-confident by using the skills of *resource development and installation*. I'll also show you how to optimise every minute you spend at work by using cutting edge time management skills.

Did you know that it takes around 21 minutes to recover your focus of attention when you are distracted? If, like most people, you work in an environment where there are constant distractions, Chapter 5 will offer you the opportunity to develop a laser-like focus of attention to achieve your goals. You'll learn about the concept of attentional focus and how you can train your brain to cut through distractions and conserve precious mental energy. I'll also share with you nutrition tips for optimum brain functioning.

Increasingly, interpersonal skills are a greater determinant of success in the workplace than knowledge or technical skills. In Chapter 6, I'll show you how to establish rapport with others effortlessly and use emotional intelligence to develop productive relationships. You'll learn about the psychology of social interaction in competitive situations and how to handle yourself. I'll also teach you a range of assertiveness techniques and tell you how to deal with aggressive or passive-aggressive behaviour in others.

In Chapter 7 I'll help you to spot the early warning signs of work-related stress before they become a problem. I'll also teach you a range of strategies that will inoculate you against stress and ensure that you maintain high levels of mental and physical well-being. In the final part of the book, I'll introduce you to *mindfulness,* a nonspiritual meditative practice that really could change your life for the better.

As with most self-help books, you may want to turn immediately to a certain chapter depending on your specific needs or inclination. Feel free to do so, although I would recommend that you read Chapter 1 first as it provides the theory that underpins all of the other approaches that follow.

I've written this book because I've spent many years studying and practicing CBT and career counselling. I'm passionate about both approaches because they have the power to transform people's lives. I really hope you find the content useful and that it will help you along the way throughout your personal journey.

Chapter 1

Introduction to cognitive and behavioural approaches to achieving career success

We have 50,000 thoughts per day[1] – not all of them are helpful

I know you've just started reading this book, but please indulge me and just take a minute to sit somewhere quiet and close your eyes. Just notice the flow of your thoughts and where they take you. You may notice visual images, memories and verbal thoughts occurring to you in completely random ways. I'd like you to also pay attention to any subtle changes in how you are feeling: notice how some of these random thoughts have an emotional tone to them. Perhaps they make you feel slightly amused, baffled, concerned? When I run this simple exercise in workshops with people, they are very often surprised to discover the level of mental activity that is taking place in their minds on a second-by-second basis. As human beings we have a tendency to take our thoughts for granted, unless we deliberately engage our minds in a specific activity. But as I hope to show you, our minds are constantly active, often below our level of awareness, responding to what's happening in the present moment but also flitting backwards and forwards between our past memories and our imagined futures. All of these mental activities will influence the way we feel and act, the view we have of ourselves, the world and other people – sometimes without our even knowing it. We can harness this amazing mental powerhouse by becoming more skilled in managing our thinking processes to achieve success in the workplace and life in general. And *Cognitive Behavioural Therapy* or *CBT* gives us the tools to do this.

Cognitive behavioural therapy simplified

C = Cognitive: All mental processes that we engage in, including our focus of attention and thoughts about the present, future and past.

These could include verbal or visual thoughts, dreams and our perceptions of the world, ourselves and others.

B = **Behavioural**: Every action we take generally following some thought process. This can involve getting things done, communicating with others and seeking pleasurable activities. But it can also include *avoiding* certain things in life or choosing *not* to carry out an action (e.g. telling your boss what you think of them when annoyed).

T = **Therapy**: A bit of a scary word as it implies mental illness, but in this instance it's helpful to think of the term as describing a systematic methodology for overcoming a specific problem.

CBT is recognised throughout the world as a cutting-edge treatment used to help people deal with a range of psychological challenges. Examples include:

- Depression
- Anxiety
- Social anxiety
- Post-traumatic stress disorder (PTSD)
- Panic disorder
- Phobias
- Obsessive compulsive disorders (OCD)
- Eating disorders
- Body dysmorphic disorders (BDD)

CBT is highly scientific and uses *evidence-based practice* in its approach. This means that the effectiveness of each method for dealing with a specific psychological problem (depression for example) is thoroughly tested through *random controlled trials*. Participants are randomly assigned to a CBT treatment group, an alternative therapy and a placebo group to prove the effectiveness of the methods used. Years of research and ongoing improvement have led CBT to be recommended by the National Institute for Health and Clinical Excellence (NICE) within the British National Health Service (NHS) for dealing with different psychological problems that millions of people experience.

At this point, I just want to emphasise that CBT approaches aren't just confined to dealing with 'mental health problems'. The origins of this highly effective therapy go back to the 1970s and the two 'founding fathers', Albert Ellis and Aaron Beck, who developed CBT specifically to help their patients overcome different psychological problems. As I mentioned, CBT has broadened its scope by developing a wide range of detailed therapeutic protocols for treating specific psychological disorders world-wide (e.g. PTSD). However, in recent years CBT has also evolved as a methodology for *optimising* that way we think, feel and act when tackling the challenges that life throws at us on a daily basis (going for job interviews, negotiating an increase in salary) without assuming that we are suffering from a psychological illness. This is largely due to the work of Martin E. P. Seligman, former president of the American Psychological Association and Professor of Psychology at the University of Pennsylvania. Seligman is widely acknowledged to be the world's leading expert in positive psychology and has adapted CBT by moving away from a 'psychological disorder' model to an approach that helps people to deal with life challenges more effectively and obtain greater levels of happiness and satisfaction. Seligman's work in this area is highly influential and he has published a number of best-selling books including *Learned Optimism* (2006), *Authentic Happiness* (2002) and *The Optimistic Child* (2007). I have followed a similar approach by combining career counselling and CBT, drawing on my experience over the years in both disciplines, and can now offer you a powerful model that will help you to succeed in your career.

As you'll come to see, one of the most important features of CBT is that once you have learned the techniques set out in this book, you will become self-sufficient in dealing with present and future challenges in your career and life. This is because CBT will help you to define emotional and behavioural challenges more clearly, for example, dealing with anxiety whilst giving a presentation, and help you to set constructive goals around how you would prefer to feel and act (e.g. confident and alert). The CBT strategies that I'll teach you will give you a problem-solving approach to managing your thoughts, feelings and actions more effectively in the workplace and life in general. But before I go any further, I want to tell you about Viktor Frankl.

Viktor Frankl

Like his contemporary Sigmund Freud, Viktor Frankl was a Jew living in Austria when the Nazis swept to power in the 1930s. He was also a psychiatrist who went on to develop a form of psychotherapy called *logotherapy*. Its central principle is that the main motivational force for human beings is the search for meaning in life. What is singularly remarkable about this man is that he developed his theories whilst suffering extreme degradation and forced labour in the death camps of Nazi Germany, including Auschwitz. Apart from his sister, Frankl's whole family died in the camps or gas chambers, including his wife. It is difficult to imagine how bleak life must have seemed for Frankl after his loved ones had died and he faced a daily regime of brutality and possible execution. And yet, even under these potentially degrading circumstances, Frankl developed what he described as the last of the human freedoms (Frankl, 1984): *the ability to choose his response to external circumstances.* Frankl used his experiences in the camps to gradually forge his mental and emotional capacities so that eventually he experienced an inner freedom that his captors could not take from him. If they stripped him naked and tried to degrade him, his chosen response was to feel dignity as a human being. When his fellow prisoners gave up their struggle by hurling themselves at the electrified fences to die, Frankl chose hope, that one day he would be free from captivity to share the knowledge he had developed in extremis.

A more recent example is that of Nelson Mandela, who was imprisoned for 28 years spent mostly on Robben Island, a former leper colony, as a consequence of his battle against apartheid. In his autobiography, *Long Walk to Freedom* (1995), Mandela describes the brutality of the Afrikaner guards, the physically punishing enforced labour and the squalid living accommodation in his cell. But, like Frankl, Mandela did not allow himself to feel degraded by this experience and chose his response to external circumstances by acting with dignity, teaching political economy to fellow prisoners and playing chess.

Frankl and Mandela are inspiring examples of the power of thought and how the human mind can be used to endure severe hardship and choose a positive response to adversity. CBT provides us with the framework to choose our own cognitive, behavioural and emotional responses to life challenges, as we shall see when we explore two important foundational models that will underpin many of the strategies set out within this book.

The life challenges model

The model set out in Figure 1.1 can be used to explore the complex interaction that occurs between our thoughts, emotions, physiology and behaviour patterns when we engage with any minor or major challenge in life. You can find a blank copy of the model at Appendix 1.

We all face challenges on a daily basis of varying magnitude. At a minor level we may be confronted by delays on the way to work or the challenge might be more significant, like giving a major presentation for a contract in a high-pressure situation. Or we may face future challenges on the horizon that preoccupy us in the present moment, like the prospect of starting a new job in another country. Within this model recognition is given to the fact that we may be *influenced* by these challenges in terms of how we think, feel and act. But just like Viktor Frankl and Nelson Mandela, we can make a big difference to the way we feel by changing unhelpful thoughts and behavioural reactions – *even if we can't change the nature of the challenge.*

Life challenges trigger *thought processes* in our minds that invariably lead to *emotional reactions* and *physiological responses.* These in turn influence our *behavioural reactions.* Once triggered, these four domains interact with one another rapidly. Imagine you are at a conference feeling fairly relaxed watching other people giving presentations. Quite unexpectedly you are called upon to give a presentation on a subject

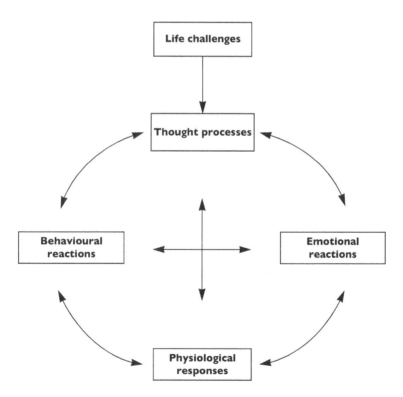

Figure 1.1 Life challenges model.

you know little of. There are a hundred people at the conference and suddenly you find yourself thinking, 'I'm really going to screw this up and look stupid'. You have a mental image of yourself red-faced and trembling in front of the audience. Your anxiety level soars and you can feel your heart thumping in your chest. You walk to the lectern in a timid way wishing you could hide behind it. Your mind has registered your defensive physical behaviour as a danger signal along with your rapidly beating heart and you start to think, 'This really is all going wrong!' leading to a further spike in anxiety.

When you apply the model to the above example you can see how this particular challenge (impromptu public speaking) triggered a negative thought process, which led in turn to an unhelpful emotional reaction (anxiety). We experience all emotions as physiological responses and in this instance the huge surge of adrenaline resulted in rapid heartbeat and sweating. This led to timid, defensive behaviour. But the process doesn't stop there, because the brain registers these physiological and behavioural changes as a potential threat, which leads to further catastrophic thinking and another loop round the vicious cycle of increased anxiety, adrenaline and deteriorating performance. Understanding how these domains interact with one another provides us with a method for analysing and improving our strategies for dealing with present and future life challenges. But before we go any further with the model, let's consider some of the thinking processes that we routinely engage in and some of the pitfalls to avoid.

Thought–feeling links

Let's go back to the example in which you are suddenly called upon to give a presentation with little preparation. You may think that the situation makes you anxious and most people believe that events make them feel a certain way (your boss being rude to you *makes* you annoyed, a car cutting in front of you *makes* you angry). But on closer examination you can see that it very often isn't the event that makes you feel a certain emotion, but the way you are thinking about it. In the example above, the prospect of giving a presentation at short notice doesn't *make* you feel anxious; telling yourself that you're going to screw it up does. The reason why most people make these thought–feeling links is because we are constantly bombarded by external events and react to them without reflection. When something challenging happens to you, it's worth pausing for a few seconds and considering your mental response. Ask yourself, is this thinking going to help or hinder me? This is what Viktor Frankl described as having the freedom to choose between what he referred to as *stimulus and response*. As we have seen, although his captors tried to break Frankl's spirit through various degrading acts (the 'stimulus'), his mental response was one of dignity. Cultivating the ability to choose your mental response to challenging situations will give you a powerful tool for dealing with adversity. Start with moderately challenging situations to begin with and consider what effect this approach has on your mood. Next time someone cuts in front of you in traffic or you are stuck in a queue, pause for a few seconds and choose your response.

Unhelpful patterns of thinking

When people constantly experience unhelpful negative emotions like anxiety and depression, they do so largely as the result engaging in unhelpful patterns of thinking. Thanks to advances in neuroscience and the use of fMRI brain scanners, we now know that our thoughts actually change the physical shape of our brains due to the activities of neurons and the connections forged between them. A dramatic example of this was demonstrated by Professor Eleanor Maguire (Maguire et al., 2000), a cognitive neuroscientist based at University College London. In 2000, Professor Maguire recruited sixteen London Black Cab drivers and used an fMRI brain scanner to discover that the back part of their hippocampuses (the part of the brain responsible for memory and spatial navigation) was significantly larger than average. Anyone familiar with London cabbies knows that they have to undertake a gruelling training and examination called 'the knowledge' in which they have to memorise the 25,000 streets in London and be able to recall routes between any one of them. This sustained mental activity led to substantial changes in the physical structure of the cabbies' brains. But this also means that the more someone engages in a negative thought process ('I'm crap at my job', 'I'm a failure') the more these negative neural pathways become strengthened in the brain – the saying that is often used in neuroscience is 'neurons that fire together, wire together'. This means that the individual concerned is likely to develop what is referred to as a *negative cognitive bias*. It is as though they view life through a distorted lens and they are more likely to see the downside of everything. This has a profound effect on the way these people make major decisions in life (e.g. within their career) because their negative bias may incline them towards self-defeating assumptions. They may misinterpret situations, judge themselves harshly and find it difficult to cope with life challenges. The good news is, however, that if we take control of our thinking, we can develop positive neural pathways and a more helpful cognitive bias. Professor Elaine Fox of Oxford University has found evidence that approaches such as CBT and *cognitive bias modification* (CBM) 'positivity training' (Fox, 2012) can bring about these positive neural changes in the brain. Even lifelong pessimists can become optimists if they use their brains in the right way.

Making interpretations

Moment by moment throughout our lives, we interpret what is happening to us through our five senses and this gives us our perception of reality. But, as Alfred Korzybski noted (1995), 'the map is not the territory'. Korzybski was a Polish American scholar who contributed to philosophy by developing a body of knowledge called *general semantics.* He argued that as human beings we can never truly know reality because our perceptions are filtered through our fallible brains. Think of the last time you were stressed or angry and how this impacted on your view of reality. Much of what happens to us in life that affects the way we feel is largely due to our perception of events and the different interpretations we make of them, sometimes inaccurately. Let's take a common example. Jenny is attending an interview for a promotion and one of the panel (whom she has never met) does not smile at all. Depending on how Jenny *interprets* the situation, she will have markedly different emotional reactions. If Jenny interprets the interviewer's behaviour as hostile and an indication that he does not like her, she is likely to feel anxious or irritable and neither emotion is conducive to presenting herself in the best light. Alternatively, she might conclude that the interviewer has a very formal style and doesn't want to give anything away. It would be impossible for her to prove whether or not he liked or disliked her at this stage, but the latter interpretation is more likely to help her maintain a calm frame of mind. Here are a number of different mental pitfalls it's worth being aware of.

All-or-nothing (or black-or-white) thinking: Absolutist thinking that often triggers intense, negative unhelpful emotions and interferes with achieving constructive goals. If Jenny tells herself that she *must* get the promotion at all costs or it will be the end of the world, she is more likely to suffer from anxiety during the interview and low mood if she is unsuccessful. If, on the other hand, Jenny engaged in *realistic* and *flexible* thinking she will take the pressure off herself and perform better. She could do this by considering the benefits of going for the interview even if she doesn't get the promotion (putting down a marker by showing that she's ambitious) and developing a back-up plan if she doesn't succeed in this instance.

Fortune-telling: This involves making negative predictions about what will happen in the future, often with very little evidence to go on. This style of thinking is habitually adopted by people who have a tendency to be pessimistic about life in general. If Jenny were to think this way about the promotion, she might predict a dire outcome even if she succeeded, imagining that she could not cope with the additional responsibility. The antidote to this pitfall is to adopt a more balanced optimistic outlook on the future, be prepared to take calculated risks and develop a *tolerance of uncertainty*. The latter is essential for career progression as a constant desire for certainty keeps people trapped within a limiting comfort zone and prevents personal growth.

Mind-reading: This is similar to making subjective *interpretations* when the information available to us is ambiguous and often results in making negative assumptions about what other people think of us and inferring negative motives in their behaviour. Prior to the interview for the promotion, Jenny notices that her line manager is less communicative than usual. If she engaged in mind-reading, Jenny might guess that he did not think she was ready for the promotion and that he regrets supporting her application. This style of thinking would increase her stress levels prior to the interview and affect her confidence on the day. A more constructive response would be for Jenny to *generate alternative reasons* for her boss' behaviour: perhaps he's finding work stressful right now and is a little preoccupied.

Emotional reasoning: This means interpreting what is happening to you based on how you are feeling emotionally. Before the interview, Jenny is feeling slightly nervous, as most people are on these occasions. Instead of accepting this as a normal part of the situation and focussing on the task in hand, Jenny interprets her feeling of nervousness as a danger signal that things are going wrong and she becomes hyper-vigilant for other dangers. That's why she is more predisposed to interpreting the interviewer's behaviour as unfriendly with the unhelpful consequence of increasing her anxiety. Our emotional responses are very powerful. They helped our ancient ancestors to survive (e.g. 'fight or flight' reactions) and we have inherited them through the process of natural selection. We rely on these emotional responses as instincts about situations and other people and they form an essential part of our decision making processes. Did you know that the word 'emotion' comes from the Latin *emovere* or *movere*, literally 'to move'? However, it's always worth bearing in mind that we need to be *guided* by our emotions and not *misled* by them. Tune into how you are feeling emotionally in a situation but then balance your emotional response with rational thinking. Ask yourself if you need to lead with your head (rational thinking) or your heart (emotional thinking) in this situation or a combination of both. For example, Jenny could rationalise that feeling nervous is normal when engaging in a challenging situation like an interview and not a 'danger signal'. She can rely on this nervous response to sharpen her mind through the additional adrenaline triggered without becoming distracted by the physical sensations of nervousness.

Overgeneralisation: Drawing 'global' conclusions from one or a few events that have occurred in your life so that they distort your perspective. Jenny has experienced sexist behaviour from a manager on a couple of occasions during her career. If she had a tendency to overgeneralise, Jenny might conclude that her industry is populated by sexist managers who will block her progress and she may feel discouraged from applying for more senior positions. In this instance, it would be more helpful for Jenny to test the accuracy of her impressions by trying to get a more balanced perspective and looking for alternative evidence. For example, she could research industry data to establish the prevalence of women managers in her particular sector. She could also join a 'women in management' networking group to obtain alternative perspectives on overcoming potential barriers to career progression.

Labelling: Similar to overgeneralising as it involves rating yourself, other people or events as completely negative. If Jenny did not achieve the promotion she aspires too, she might label herself as a 'failure', the management team as 'bastards' because they appointed someone else and the industry she works in as an 'unfair place'. The problem with labelling is that it leads to a harsh, distorted perspective of oneself and others and does not take sufficient account of *human fallibility* and the possibility that we are all capable of change and improvement. If we don't achieve success in one endeavour, it doesn't logically follow that we are a total failure and it's helpful to consider past successes to counter this negative way of thinking. Jenny, for example, could reflect on the fact that she achieved success by getting her current job even if she didn't obtain a promotion this time.

Making demands: Rigid thinking that doesn't leave room for different outcomes or points of view. You can tell if you or others are engaged in this type of thinking when you notice the use of absolutist language and terms such as *should, must, got to, have to*. Albert Ellis (1913–2007) is credited as having created the first form of CBT (Neenan & Dryden, 2011) in the 1950s that he named rational emotive behaviour therapy (REBT). According to Ellis, our tendency to make demands of ourselves, others and life in general is one of the main reasons that we experience emotional problems and his therapy emphasises countering this unhelpful response to life challenges. If Jenny believes that she absolutely *must* get the promotion (because she needs the money, wants the status, etc.), she will be more likely to increase the amount of pressure she places on herself and, crucially, the amount of anxiety she will experience. This combination of increased pressure and anxiety risks undermining Jenny's performance at the interview and if she fails to obtain the promotion, she is more likely to experience a crushing sense of failure that will leave her feeling hopeless and demotivated. This type of thinking is common in people who have perfectionistic tendencies and crave certainty and control and can often lead to them experiencing high levels of stress and missed deadlines. Although it's reasonable to aim at high standards, making demands that you *have* to achieve a specific outcome can bring about the failure you most seek to avoid. Demanding that you *must* achieve an erection or fall asleep because you have a busy day ahead is almost guaranteed to be counterproductive. Ellis recommended *holding flexible preferences* about ourselves, other people and the world as a way of countering the tendency to make rigid demands. He characterised these preferences by using terms such as *prefer, want* and *wish*. This doesn't mean to say that you cannot be highly motivated to achieve a certain standard and have a very strong but flexible preference (that you really want the promotion or wish to deliver a high quality presentation). By thinking flexibly you maintain high standards and ambition whilst recognising the possibility of a different outcome to the one preferred. This has the effect of reducing unhelpful stress and enabling constructive contingency planning so that you have an alternative course of action to fall back on.

Mental filtering/discounting the positive: This process involves taking on board any evidence that supports a negative belief someone holds about themselves, other people and the world in general. It also involves discounting any evidence that contradicts the negative belief. Let's take Jenny's situation as an example. If she has developed a negative belief

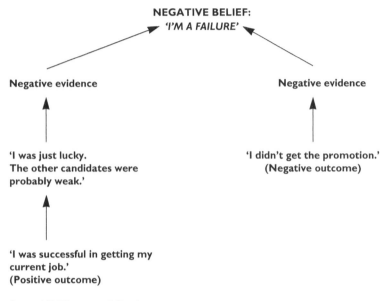

Figure 1.2 The mental filtering process.

about herself ('I'm a failure'), Jenny will be more inclined to take note of negative evidence that supports her belief (Figure 1.2). In this instance, if she failed to obtain the promotion, she would accept this as further proof that she is a failure. But it doesn't stop there. Even when something positive happens to Jenny, she has a tendency to convert these events into yet further negative evidence to support her self-denigrating belief. So when she gets a job she has applied for, instead of congratulating herself on this achievement, Jenny discounts the positive outcome and turns it into a negative ('I was just lucky – the other candidates were probably weak').

This type of mental filtering is extremely unhelpful in terms of eroding self-confidence as it often occurs without the person being aware of the process – it just happens automatically. Also, it's a cumulative process in which negative evidence gets filtered in regularly, constantly feeding the negative belief as it grows in strength and magnitude. We'll explore the role of **core beliefs** in more detail later on in this chapter.

Low frustration tolerance: Believing that you can't tolerate the discomfort that's involved in pursuing a worthwhile goal rather than thinking that the long-term gain is worth the short-term pain. Low frustration tolerance, or LFT, manifests itself in a number of ways but its key characteristics include difficulty in enduring short-term physical, emotional and psychological discomfort in pursuit of a positive goal. Engaging in this way of thinking represents one of the greatest barriers to achievement in life for many people because it keeps them trapped within a comfort zone that continues to shrink. Examples include:

- Avoiding applying for senior jobs that require more responsibility due to fear of failure
- Procrastinating when faced with a lengthy piece of work that will be mentally demanding
- Needing deadlines and increased stress as a motivation to take action
- Avoiding giving presentations and being the focus of attention because of the anxiety this causes
- Failing to follow a diet or physical exercise regime because of the discomfort involved
- Putting off further study for career progression because it seems far too exhausting 'on top of the day job'

Think about your greatest accomplishments in life and the effort you had to make to achieve these successes. I'm willing to bet that you had to pay a price by enduring some discomfort along the way.

If you can develop a *high frustration tolerance* philosophy for work and life in general, you will stand a much greater chance of achieving success. It isn't easy but it is effective. In the same way that you subject yourself to physical rigour in the gym in order to gain increased muscle and stamina, regularly engaging in activities that require you to tolerate some level of physical and mental discomfort will enable you to develop 'psychological muscle'. You could think of it as a **'resilience bank account'**: every time you willingly engage in a challenging activity that requires discomfort but leads to achievement, you make a deposit. You could apply this principle in many domains, from completing a report that you have been putting off to sky-diving for charity. On the other side of the equation, every time you engage in avoidant or self-indulgent behaviour (watching TV for hours whilst snacking, putting off physical exercise), you make a withdrawal from the account. In this way, you can build up credit to 'earn' your treats – they're far more enjoyable with a clear conscience. Michael Neenan refers to this stoic approach as 'discomfort practice' in his excellent book, *Developing resilience: a cognitive-behavioural approach* (2009) and provides a wide range of techniques for developing resilience in the workplace. It's helpful if you can practise *high frustration tolerance* regularly and consistently. Think of everyday situations that you can turn into personal victories (such as getting out of bed when the alarm goes off rather than pressing the snooze button; avoiding that sugary snack with coffee during the afternoon). If you can exercise strength during these daily but overlooked trials, you will find the bigger challenges in life easier to deal with.

Personalising: Believing that when other people act in a negative way or things go wrong that you are being personally held to account. This causes a great deal of stress as individuals who personalise take on the burden of responsibility for events that are often beyond their control and they experience needless feelings of guilt or hurt. They may have attended meetings where colleagues are more tense than usual in the way they speak and act. Or they may have received a group email from a senior manager expressing concern about the team's performance. In both instances, individuals who personalise will be more likely to assume that they are somehow to blame even if they had done nothing to offend colleagues at the meeting and their personal performance is on target. The best approach for countering this tendency to personalise is to *explore different reasons* for other people's behaviour and events that occur by separating yourself from the situation and examining the evidence objectively. Did the people at the meeting who were tense focus on you alone or were they like that with everyone? Why would a senior manager imply a criticism of you personally when your performance is good? Are they just reacting to pressure and firing off an email to everyone to relieve their own stress?

Now that you've gained an understanding of common thinking errors, make a note of any that you commonly experience and make a conscious effort to use the counter-strategies I've described when you recognise that you are falling into unhelpful responses. Also, don't give yourself a hard time if you recognise that you make one or more of the thinking errors I've described. We *all* have a tendency to fall into these mental traps. Being aware of this tendency is the first step to changing negative thinking patterns and developing positive alternative neural pathways.

I'm going to teach you two important methods for carrying out *formulations* and it will be helpful for you to refer back to the list of thinking errors to support you in this process. A formulation is a method for analysing how you respond to challenging situations in the work place or your personal life. It will help you to gain a better understanding of how you think, feel and act in different situations and this analysis will help you to develop optimum strategies for achieving your goals in life, no matter what they are.

Carrying out a life challenge formulation

If you've read this far, I hope that one of the key messages you're getting from this book is that *you have the power to manage the way you think* and consequently, the way you feel and act. Only human beings have the ability to think about their thoughts – this is referred to in psychological literature as **meta-cognition**. This means that when you find yourself faced with a challenging situation and you feel under pressure, you have the ability to stand back from your responses and examine them rather than simply *reacting* to circumstances in the same way that an animal does. Developing this ability can be incredibly empowering as it provides you with the freedom to choose your response to the challenges that life throws up, as Viktor Frankl showed us through his example. Let's start this process by carrying out a life challenge formulation together.

1   I'd like you to recall a recent situation that you found quite challenging in some way. It could have been something that you experienced at work or in your personal life. In order to get a more vivid recollection of what happened, close your eyes and go back to the event as though you are actually experiencing it right now. Immerse yourself: what can you see, hear, smell, feel or taste?

2   Describe what you consider to be the most challenging aspect of the situation in the 'Life Challenges' box on the diagram (Figure 1.3).

3   Summarise what was going through your mind in the 'Thought Processes' box. What were the key thoughts that the challenging situation triggered?

4   Now enter any feelings that you experienced in the 'Emotional Reactions' box. Make a note in particular of any emotions that felt uncomfortable as part of the experience, for example, anxiety or anger.

5   When you experienced these emotions, what sort of physical sensations did you experience (e.g. increased heartbeat, rapid breathing, muscular tension)? Enter these sensations in the 'Physical Response' box.

6   Finally, describe how you acted (or didn't act) in the 'Behavioural Reactions' box. How did your thoughts, emotions and physical sensations influence your behaviour?

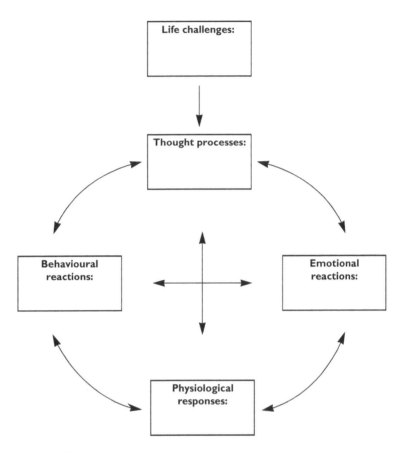

Figure 1.3 The life challenges formulation.

Well done! You've just completed your first formulation. We'll be returning to this model throughout the book and you'll gain experience of using it in various situations to gain more control over your thought processes when dealing with challenges.

Now that you know how to carry out a life challenges formulation, I'd like to introduce you to the **ABC model** as a different approach to diagnosing optimum thinking strategies to help you attain your goals.

The ABC model

The ABC model is similar to the life challenges formulation in terms of providing you with a framework for analysing any psychological or behavioural barriers that stand in the way of you achieving your career or life goals. Once you have determined these barriers, the ABC model will help you to develop effective strategies for achieving your goals. Let's have a quick overview of the model to see how it works. We'll then explore each component in detail.

'**A**' = **activating event**: Something specific about a situation, whether in the present, future or past, that seizes our attention and acts as a *trigger* on our thoughts. 'A' is also described as 'Adversity' in CBT literature to convey the notion of challenges that need to be overcome.

'**B**' = **belief**: This can mean the deeper core beliefs that we form in child-hood. 'B' is also shorthand for any cognitive activities that are triggered by the *activating event*, including automatic thoughts, visual images, memories and personal meanings that people attach to the event.

'**C**' = **consequences**: Emotional, physical and behavioural consequences that are triggered by thoughts at 'B' like a chain reaction.

Another way of viewing the model is as the formula:

$$A \times B = C$$

This is because the greater the intensity of the activating event at 'A', the more profound the emotional, behavioural and physical conse-quences experienced at 'C'. 'B' – or our thought processes – mediates between what happens to us and how we feel and act in response to the situation. Our thinking may be unhelpful in that it *magnifies* the nature of the challenge creating a sense of threat, or we may think in a balanced, helpful way resulting in calm, constructive action. Now that you have an overview, let's look at each component of the model in more detail.

Component 'A'

As I mentioned above, 'A' represents something specific about a situ-ation that seizes your attention and triggers a thinking process in your mind. As human beings we are constantly bombarded by sights, sounds and tactile stimuli as we go about our daily business. If we paid close attention to everything that happened to us, our minds would soon become overwhelmed, so our attention is in a constant state of periph-eral flux, enabling us to function without our neural circuitry becoming overloaded. If you've ever driven a car in heavy traffic, you will have experienced this process. Your attention to the flow of traffic around you and the act of driving is evenly spread. Your focus is constantly switching between what other drivers are doing around you whilst you change gear, indicate, accelerate or brake. Suddenly the traffic lights change to amber and your attention is fully focussed on one thing in your overall environment. It triggers a very rapid thought that you need to stop the car which in turn leads to an emotional consequence of raised concern followed by a behavioural consequence of applying the brakes. This is just one example of how your attention is on 'autopilot' until it focuses on a specific 'A'. We can also make a distinction between 'A's that are, objectively speaking, *actual events* and 'A's that are subjective *inferred events*. Let me give you an example.

John receives a call from his manager who wants to meet with him urgently. When they meet, John's manager tells him in no uncertain terms that he is very unhappy with the report John has written recently and draws his attention to a number of errors. He tells John that he expects him to resubmit the report by the end of the week with the corrections or he will mark him down at his monthly appraisal meeting. If we apply the ABC model to John's situation, we can see that his manager's warning is an *actual event* at 'A' (he left him in no doubt as to the consequences) and this triggered thoughts about the risk of receiving a poor appraisal at 'B', which in turn caused John to have feelings of concern at 'C'.

Inferred events are subtly different as they result in us making subjective interpretations of what is happening and can be described as hunches or 'gut feelings' that go beyond the evidence that is available to us and may or may not be a correct reading of the situation. Let's take Karen's situation as an example.

Karen's organisation has won a contract to deliver care for the elderly within a local community area and she has been charged with managing the project. The decision to award the contract to a commercial company with a board of shareholders rather than a local charity has caused some criticism in the local media and Karen is due to give the keynote speech at the launch event. Karen is about to give her presentation when she notices a well-dressed elderly woman in the front row who seems to have a disapproving expression on her face. At this point Karen begins to imagine that the women will direct a verbal attack at her organisation and starts to feel apprehensive. She notices that her stomach has begun churning and her mouth feels very dry. Just before she begins her presentation, Karen reaches for a glass of water and knocks it over her written notes.

In this instance Karen's 'A' was an *inference* that the elderly women's facial expression spelled trouble and was a sign of a forthcoming verbal attack. But this was Karen's subjective interpretation of the event, as she didn't have unequivocal evidence to support her gut feeling – after all, the woman could have been suffering from some physical discomfort or was merely concentrating intently. What's significant in this example is that Karen's inference at 'A' triggered a disturbing thought at 'B' which led to a range of unhelpful emotional, behavioural and physiological consequences at 'C'.

It's worth pointing out that 'A's can also act as *internal triggers* as well as external events. Initially, the elderly woman's facial expression was an external trigger that led to Karen making unhelpful interpretations about the event. But let's say that the woman adopted a more neutral expression, Karen may still have focussed on her churning stomach and dry mouth and these internal triggers could have prompted the thought that she was about to dry up in front of the audience during her presentation, leading to even greater feelings of anxiety. Physical sensations often act as internal triggers along with emotions, as I've described previously in the section on *emotional reasoning*.

Critical 'A's can act as triggers in *past, present* and *future* events. We had an example of the elderly woman's expression acting as a trigger in the present. But when Karen's boss gave her the task of preparing for the presentation, this may have triggered anxious thoughts in Karen's mind about a hostile audience in the future. Or it could equally have brought to mind past presentations Karen had made being on the receiving end of angry audience members.

Component 'B'

'B' stands for 'beliefs' within the ABC model, that is to say subjective beliefs you may have about the situation based on previous experiences. 'B' also represents any cognitive processes that get triggered by an *activating event* at 'A'. For example, when something happens to you, you will probably experience fleeting thoughts, visual images or memories from the past. Your thoughts will often be neutral and below your level of awareness because cognitive processing happens so rapidly. Often you will have positive and constructive thoughts but occasionally you may engage in unhelpful modes of thinking. These can be categorised as follows.

Negative automatic thoughts (NATs): I mentioned earlier that we have approximately 50,000 thoughts each day and not all of them are helpful. NATs are similar to the annoying insects (gnats) that buzz around your head. They occur spontaneously, often when we find ourselves in stressful situations. They include all of the unhelpful patterns of thinking that we considered earlier and will almost always have a detrimental effect on our mood. The problem with NATs is that they are very seductive, as they seem believable ('I messed up that presentation – I'm an idiot!'). And one negative thought usually leads to another ('If I keep screwing up like this, they'll probably get rid of me'). But we only reap the negative consequences of NATs because we *pay attention* to them. If we challenge NATs or ignore them, we starve them of attention and prevent them from disturbing us.

Underlying assumptions and rules: Although you may not be aware of it, you have probably developed a number of unspoken rules or assumptions that act as guiding principles in your career and life in general – you could call them *rules for living*. They might include standards of behaviour and quality that you insist on for yourself in the workplace. For example, some people have high standards that they impose on themselves around punctuality and they make sure that they're five minutes early for every meeting as they believe that this denotes respect to others and professionalism. These rules and principles may serve us well and they can act as a moral compass to guide us through life during turbulent times. However, if our rules for living become too rigid they are highly likely to cause us stress if their conditions aren't met. This is a common problem for people with perfectionistic standards who live by the rule that their work 'must always be of the highest standard'. If these individuals are put into a situation where they are required to produce a high output of average quality work to tight deadlines, they often find it difficult to compromise their high standards and risk burnout trying to maintain them. Underlying assumptions and rules are closely related to core beliefs.

Core beliefs: In early childhood we all develop ideas about ourselves, other people and the world and this perspective of reality can be described in terms of *core beliefs* that we hold (Beck, 2011). We are born with a certain temperament largely inherited from our parents (Young and Klosko, 1994) but our early environment, particularly family, will influence our development (often described as 'nature versus nurture'). Early childhood experiences can have a profound effect on our core beliefs and if some of these experiences are negative, they may lead to the individual developing associated negative core beliefs about themselves, others and the world in general. Let's look at some examples.

Mark

Mark was an only child and grew up in a strict family environment. His parents were well-intentioned and wanted him to succeed in education, particularly as he was their only child. But no matter how hard Mark tried at school, he could never meet the high standards set by his parents.

Mark's core belief: 'I'm not good enough'.

Amanda

Amanda grew up in a loving, supportive family, the second eldest of three sisters. Her parents encouraged her to do well at school without pressuring her and they also nurtured a spirit of adventure in her. Amanda learned to develop confidence by taking on new challenges that took her outside of her comfort zone but she knew that she could always return to the safety of the family.

Amanda's core belief: 'I'm OK and most other people are OK'.

Colin

Colin's parents were very cold towards him, his brother and each other. He was rarely shown physical affection, like hugs or kisses, and his parents rarely showed their emotions. In later life he realised that they had both suffered from depression but had thought that he had been in some way responsible for their lack of affection when he was a child.

Colin's core belief: 'I'm unlikable'.

Generally speaking, most people won't even realise that they have 'core beliefs' as the way they view themselves, others and the world is just 'the way it is' – their reality. Also, these beliefs can remain deep below the surface and are only noticed when triggered by an event, similar to driving over a bump in the road. So Colin, for example, doesn't go around all day telling himself, 'I'm unlikable'. But if he starts work at a new company and feels the need to develop professional relationships in a competitive environment, he may feel awkward and lacking in confidence which is an indication that Colin's core belief has been activated. And because experiencing these negative core beliefs is an emotionally painful experience (Colin feels anxiety and shame when he thinks this way), many people unknowingly avoid situations where there is a danger that they will be triggered. So in Colin's case, he instinctively avoids social gatherings inside and outside of work because he is automatically (and often unconsciously) scanning for evidence that will confirm his negative core belief (ambiguous facial expressions and body language). Without him even being aware of it, Colin's negative core belief is driving his behaviour and determining the direction his life will take.

Falling into these self-defeating patterns of behaviour that are belief-driven is a process referred to by the psychologist Jeffrey E. Young as *'life traps'* (Young & Klosko, 1994). Even if you don't hold anything like the negative beliefs that I've just described, it's worth pausing for a moment and considering if you hold *any* views about yourself that may be unhelpful in your career or life in general. Try the following brief exercise.

1   Identify any unhelpful views you may hold about yourself.
2   Consider how you developed these views of yourself during childhood.
3   Describe a positive, alternative way of thinking about yourself that counters any negative beliefs.

The key to combating negative beliefs and mental filtering is to continually gather *alternative positive counter-evidence.* I've mentioned that the way we can reshape our minds is by developing helpful neural pathways – every time you internalise a positive piece of evidence that counters a negative belief whilst supporting a positive, alternative way of thinking, you strengthen that neural pathway. And one of the most effective ways of doing this is to keep a **positive data log**. The format doesn't matter: you can use a paper notebook, a tablet, your laptop or mobile. The important thing is that you get into the discipline of recording positive evidence that will weaken any unhelpful beliefs whilst strengthening the alternative positive view of yourself *no matter how small the evidence is.* This may seem laborious and unremarkable, but it is a highly effective way of forcing your brain to register positive evidence and improve your self-confidence.

Component 'C'

As I mentioned earlier, 'C' stands for the emotional, behavioural and physiological consequences that get triggered by our thoughts and/or beliefs at 'B' followed by an activating event at 'A'. I'll unpack this part of the model in more detail by introducing the *emotions table* that outlines the behavioural, physical and cognitive consequences of our thinking styles or beliefs. But before I do that, I want to explain the role of helpful and unhelpful negative emotions and how they interact with one another.

Helpful ☺ versus unhelpful ☹ <u>negative</u> emotions

I have deliberately underlined the word 'negative' above because it seems contradictory at first and you may have thought, 'How can a *negative* emotion be helpful in any way? Also, what about *positive* emotions?' The reason I'm focussing on negative emotions (e.g. the ones you don't necessarily enjoy experiencing) is because the main aim of this book is to help you succeed in your career and taking that path will inevitably require you to overcome a number of challenges along the way to achieving your goals. Experiencing positive emotions such as *joy* or *enthusiasm* rarely causes a problem unless we become addicted to them to the distraction of all else. But if we find ourselves in challenging situations, like competing for a job or working to tight deadlines, we are highly likely to experience negative emotions and how we deal with them can make the difference between success or failure. As you'll see later in this book, it's far more helpful for you to experience *concern* when you're in a high-pressure situation – like attending a job interview – than *anxiety*, which may impair your performance. I'll show you how to *think* and *act* constructively when facing challenges so that you're more likely to experience helpful rather than unhelpful negative emotions.

Emotional processes and how they interact

As you can see from the diagram (Figure 1.4), our thoughts, emotions, behavioural reactions and physiological responses are intricately linked with one another. Whenever you experience an emotion, a complex internal process is set in motion.

Thoughts and images flow through your mind and you may recall memories from past events. Your attention focuses internally on physical and mental sensations or externally on your environment. You may also feel impulses to act in a certain way. Consider the following example: You're at a conference and required to give a presentation on short notice with little time to prepare. Focussing your attention on things that might go wrong with the presentation will undoubtedly increase the likelihood of anxious thoughts passing through your mind and you may even think back to previous occasions when your attempts at public speaking were unsuccessful. Drinking coffee to sharpen your mind will also increase the amount of adrenaline in your bloodstream and add to the physical

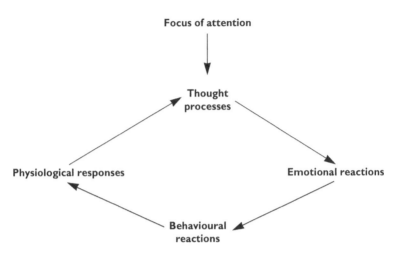

Figure 1.4 Interaction of emotional processes.

sensations of nervousness. If you behave in a fearful manner by adopting a defensive posture, your mind will register this behavioural reaction as a threat and set in motion a further increase in anxiety.

If you are able to understand this interactive process and recognise when it is taking place within you, you will be more able to recognise that you are experiencing unhelpful negative emotions and their physiological and behavioural consequences. Mentally taking stock in this way, or *decentring*, is immensely powerful as it enables you to stand back from your feelings rather than get carried away by them. As I mentioned, it's inevitable that we will experience unhelpful negative emotions at some stage when we're under pressure. If you are able to recognise these feelings as they take hold and then change the way you think and act, you are far more likely to experience *helpful* negative emotions that will increase your chances of succeeding in challenging situations.

Differentiating between helpful and unhelpful negative emotions is quite subtle in practice so to make things easy, I've set out a comprehensive list for you in Table 1.1. You may wonder why I have included certain emotions within the table and what their relevance is to achieving career success. I wanted to provide you with the full range of negative emotions for the sake of completeness and also because you *may* experience them at some stage in your career or life in general.

Table 1.1 Helpful and unhelpful negative emotions

Emotion	Type of belief	Theme	Thoughts	Behaviour
Anxiety	Unhelpful Rigid or extreme	Threat or danger	**Focus of attention:** *You monitor the threat or danger excessively and:* • Overestimate the size of the threat and create an even worse threat in your mind • Underestimate your ability to manage the situation constructively and cope with the threat • Allow thoughts about the threat to interfere with your ability to think about taking constructive action • Misinterpret physical symptoms of anxiety (e.g. increased adrenaline) as signs that the situation is becoming increasingly threatening	*You either carry out or feel like:* • Physically retreating from the situation • Mentally withdrawing from the situation (e.g. zoning out, being in denial) • Engaging in superstitious behaviours and rituals to prevent something bad from happening • Trying to numb feelings of anxiety by drinking alcohol or taking drugs • Seeking reassurance from other people that nothing bad will happen *You also find it difficult to tolerate physical symptoms of anxiety like increased heartbeat and rapid breathing*
Concern	Helpful Flexible and preferential	Threat or danger	**Focus of attention:** *You only see threats where they actually exist and:* • Estimate the threat realistically • Objectively calculate your ability to deal with the threat • Get the threat in perspective without magnifying it in your mind • Think constructively about how you are going to deal with the threat without being distracted by worrying thoughts	*You either carry out or feel like:* • Confronting the threat head-on • Tackling the threat in a constructive manner • Resisting the temptation to seek reassurance from others and rely on your own capability • Acting with confidence even if you don't feel it • Willingly tolerating the slightly uncomfortable physical sensations of concern (e.g. increased heartbeat and rapid breathing) without being distracted by them

(continued)

Table 1.1 Helpful and unhelpful negative emotions (continued)

Emotion	Type of belief	Theme	Thoughts	Behaviour
			• Interpret physical symptoms of concern as slightly uncomfortable but not a sign that the situation is becoming even more threatening • Try to discern some positive aspects within the situation and consider what you can gain from engaging in the challenge	
Depression	Unhelpful Rigid or extreme	Loss (with implications for future) Failure	**Focus of attention:** *You brood on past losses, failures or personal flaws and:* • Think of all the other losses and failures over the course of your life • Are only able to discern negative aspects to past losses and failures • Judge yourself negatively for any losses or failures and see them as a reflection of your overall character • Constantly brood on problems that can't be solved • Consider yourself to be helpless in life • Notice all the negative events happening in the world (e.g. murders, terrorist atrocities) • See the future through a glass darkly as bleak and hopeless	*You either carry out or feel like:* • Withdrawing from the company of other people and becoming increasingly isolated • Becoming less physically active • Withdrawing into yourself • Creating a gloomy environment at home that's an outward reflection of your mood • Neglecting your appearance, well-being and home environment • Trying to lift your mood in unhelpful, self-destructive ways (e.g. drinking alcohol excessively, taking street drugs, binge eating or constant grazing, spending excessively)

Emotion	Type of belief	Theme	Thoughts	Behaviour
Sadness	Helpful Flexible and preferential	Loss (with implications for future) Failure	**Focus of attention:** *You pay attention to problems that can be solved, consider your personal strengths and skills and:* • Maintain a balanced view of losses and failures, discerning some positive aspects • Engage in practical problem solving rather than constant rumination • Focus on your positive attributes and resources and think about yourself in a compassionate way in light of any losses or failures • Obtain a balanced perspective of world events discerning both the negative and the positive • Look to the future with hope and optimism in spite of the loss or failure	*You either carry out or feel like:* • Confiding in friends or family about your feelings of loss or failure, helping you to process these negative events • Taking care of your appearance, personal well-being and home environment • Acting according to a plan and not a mood by engaging in helpful routines *even if you don't feel like it* • Engaging in activities that will give a you a sense of pleasure and achievement • Recognising and avoiding self-destructive behaviours that give short-term gratification but lead to a deterioration in mood over time • Engaging in self-soothing activities and being compassionate with yourself
Anger	Unhelpful Rigid or extreme	Frustration Personal rule is broken Self-esteem is threatened	**Focus of attention:** *You perceive bad intentions and motives in other people, focus on offensive behaviour and:* • Have very rigid attitudes (e.g. 'everyone should respect me') • Assume other people meant to offend you and acted deliberately	*You either carry out or feel like:* • Attacking the other person physically or verbally • Raising your voice • Using aggressive body language and gestures (e.g. finger pointing and eyeballing)

(continued)

Table 1.1 Helpful and unhelpful negative emotions (continued)

Emotion	Type of belief	Theme	Thoughts	Behaviour
			• Consider yourself as 100 per cent right and the other person 100 per cent wrong in any argument or other adversarial situation • Find it difficult to empathise with the other person • Plan or fantasise about taking revenge on the other person	• Taking out your anger on other people or inanimate objects (e.g. kicking the chair, throwing things) • Acting in a passive-aggressive way toward the other person (e.g. 'stonewalling' them or sulking) • Withdrawing from the situation in an aggressive manner (e.g. slamming the door) • Trying to turn other people against the person who has offended you
Annoyance	Helpful Flexible and preferential	Frustration Personal rule is broken Self-esteem is threatened	**Focus of attention:** *You try to find evidence that the other person didn't wish to cause you offence and:* • Have flexible attitudes in your dealings with others (e.g. 'no one's perfect') • Consider the possibility that the other person didn't mean to offend you • Accept that both the other person and you might be right about certain aspects of the argument or adversarial situation	*You either carry out or feel like:* • Asserting yourself with the other person without becoming physically or verbally aggressive • Speaking in a calm, moderate tone of voice • Requesting rather than demanding that the other person moderate their offensive behaviour • Using calm, nonaggressive body language and gestures

Emotion	Type of belief	Theme	Thoughts	Behaviour
			• Manage to see things from the point of view of the other person • Think of how you can obtain a compromise with the other person	• Staying in the situation and working with the other person to resolve matters
Guilt	Unhelpful	Moral code or personal rule is broken by failing to do something or committing a 'sin'	**Focus of attention:** *You look for evidence of being punished for your transgression or that others are blaming you and:* • Think that you have definitely done something bad • Assume that you alone are 100 per cent responsible for the situation	*You either carry out or feel like:* • Begging other people to forgive you • Trying to displace feelings of guilt in unhelpful ways (e.g. becoming angry about what has happened and accusing others) • Promising yourself and others (unrealistically) that 'it will never happen again'
	Rigid or extreme	Hurts the feelings of a significant other	• Judge yourself according to very rigid rules or standards • Fail to take into account other people's roles in what has happened • Fail to take into account mitigating factors for the situation • Believe that you deserve to be punished in some way for what has happened	• Punishing yourself in some way, either physically or mentally • Acting in denial about what you have done to avoid experiencing the painful feelings of guilt

(continued)

Table 1.1 Helpful and unhelpful negative emotions (continued)

Emotion	Type of belief	Theme	Thoughts	Behaviour
Remorse	Helpful	Moral code or personal rule is broken by failing to do something or committing a 'sin' Flexible and preferential	Hurts the feelings of a significant other	**Focus of attention:** *You don't look for evidence that you are being punished or that others are blaming you and:* • Reflect on your behaviour in the context of the situation, taking all factors into account before making a judgement that you have transgressed • Take personal responsibility for your role in the situation • Attribute an appropriate amount of responsibility to other people involved in the situation • Evaluate your behaviour in the light of reasonable rules and standards • Take into account all mitigating factors for what happened • Regard yourself compassionately as a fallible human being rather than someone who deserves punishment	*You either carry out or feel like:* • Accepting the discomfort that accompanies the knowledge that you have done something wrong • Asking other people to forgive you without prostrating yourself • Reflecting on what you have done wrong and learning from the experience for future reference • Making appropriate amends to others for any wrong you have done them • Owning up to what you have done without acting defensively

Emotion	Type of belief	Theme	Thoughts	Behaviour
Shame	Unhelpful	Shameful personal information has been publically revealed by self or others	**Focus of attention:** *You infer reproach from others where none exists and:* • Overestimate the shamefulness of your behaviour or what has been revealed about you • Overestimate the level of importance others will attach to your behaviour or the information that has been revealed about you	*You either carry out or feel like:* • Avoiding other people because you are afraid of their disapproval • Overcompensating by attacking the people you believe to have 'shamed' you in an attempt to save face • Trying to protect your self-esteem by acting in unhelpful, self-defeating ways (e.g. acting as though you don't care what others think)
	Rigid or extreme	Others will look down upon or shun you	• Overestimate the amount of disapproval you will receive from other people • Overestimate how long others will hold you in disapproval	• Ignoring attempts by other people to ease the situation and restore normality
Regret	Helpful	Shameful personal information has been publically revealed by self or others	**Focus of attention:** *You focus on evidence that you are still accepted within the group in spite of what has happened or been revealed about you and:* • View yourself compassionately in spite of what has happened or been revealed about you • Estimate realistically how much importance others will attach to your behaviour or what has been revealed	*You either carry out or feel like:* • Engaging with other people in your social or work group rather than avoiding them • Responding positively to any attempts to restore normality • Acting unapologetically and with dignity
	Flexible and preferential	Others will look down upon or shun you	• Maintain a balanced view on the amount of disapproval you will receive from others and how long it will last	

(continued)

Table 1.1 Helpful and unhelpful negative emotions (continued)

Emotion	Type of belief	Theme	Thoughts	Behaviour
Hurt	Unhelpful Rigid or extreme	Other person treats you badly (undeserving)	**Focus of attention:** *You look for evidence that the other person doesn't care about you and:* • Overestimate how unfair the other person is being towards you • Believe that the other person doesn't care about you at all • Regard yourself as misunderstood, alone and treated unfairly ('poor me') • Ruminate on past 'hurts' that the other person has inflicted on you • Think that the other person should make the first move to put things right without you having to say anything	*You either carry out or feel like:* • Stopping speaking to the other person and sulking • Acting in a passive-aggressive way by punishing the other person through silence or criticism • Communicating that you are offended in an ambiguous way (e.g. through body language or tone of voice) without explicitly saying what you are hurt about
Disappointment	Helpful Flexible and preferential	Other person treats you badly (undeserving)	**Focus of attention:** *You look for evidence that the other person does care and:* • Realistically estimate just how unfair the other person is being toward you • Consider that the other person may have acted badly but that they probably still care about you • Don't regard yourself as a passive victim, alone and misunderstood	*You either carry out or feel like:* • Telling the other person how you feel about the situation in a straightforward and direct manner • Acting assertively if necessary without resorting to passive-aggressive behaviour • Trying to persuade the other person to act in a more considerate manner

Emotion	Type of belief	Theme	Thoughts	Behaviour
			• Avoid the temptation to dredge up other past 'hurts' • Think about taking the initiative to improve the situation between you and the other person	
Jealousy	Unhelpful Rigid or extreme	Threat to relationship with partner from another person	**Focus of attention**: *You are constantly on the lookout for threats to your relationship and:* • Perceive threats to the relationship where none exist • Overestimate threats to the relationship from other people • Believe that your partner is always on the point of leaving you for another person • Create visual images in your mind of your partner being unfaithful • Believe that your partner will leave you for another if they admit finding them attractive	*You either carry out or feel like:* • Constantly seeking reassurance from your partner that they love you and will not leave • Monitoring your partner's behaviour • Continually looking out for evidence of infidelity • Controlling your partner's activities, particularly with other people • Setting 'tests' that your partner has to pass to prove their commitment • Attacking your partner for imagined infidelities • Acting passive-aggressively (e.g. sulking)

(continued)

Table 1.1 Helpful and unhelpful negative emotions (continued)

Emotion	Type of belief	Theme	Thoughts	Behaviour
Concern for Relationship	Helpful Flexible and preferential	Threat to relationship with partner from another person	**Focus of attention:** *You allow your partner freedom within the relationship without constantly monitoring for signs of infidelity and:* • Don't perceive threats to the relationship where none exist • Don't regard your partner's interactions with others as suspicious • Don't visualise your partner committing infidelities • Accept that your partner will find others attractive without perceiving this as a threat to the relationship	*You either carry out or feel like:* • Accepting expressions of love and affection without constantly seeking reassurance • Allowing your partner freedom within the relationship without monitoring their behaviour, whereabouts and communication • Allowing your partner to show an interest in other men and women without thinking that it will lead to infidelity
Unhealthy Envy	Unhelpful Rigid or extreme	Another person possesses and enjoys something desirable that you don't have	**Focus of attention:** *You constantly think about how to obtain the desired possession at all costs, regardless of the consequences and:* • Think about the possession or its owner in a negative way to reduce its attraction to you • Pretend you're happy with what you've got when secretly you're discontent and envious	*You either carry out or feel like:* • Denigrating the other person who possesses what you desire • Denigrating the desired possession • Trying to deprive the other person of the possession • Ruining or damaging the possession to deprive the other person

Emotion	Type of belief	Theme	Thoughts	Behaviour
			• Think about ways of obtaining the possession even if it's of little use to you • Fantasise about depriving the other person of the possession	
Healthy Envy	Helpful Flexible and preferential	Another person possesses and enjoys something desirable that you don't have	**Focus of attention:** *You think about how to obtain the desired possession after considering the consequences for yourself and others and:* • Admit to yourself that you desire the possession • Admit that you're not happy with your own possession, if that's the case • Think about ways of obtaining the possession for positive reasons • Allow the other person to enjoy their possession without malice	*You either carry out or feel like:* • Seeking to obtain the possession if it's your true desire

How to use the emotions table

The following section will help you to understand the individual components of the emotions table.

Emotion and type of belief

The table contains pairs of emotions that are either *helpful* or *unhelpful* to you in achieving your goals, particularly if you experience them in challenging, stressful situations. For example, it would be unhelpful for you to experience *anxiety* if you were about to give a major presentation or attend a job interview because this emotion will undermine your mental and physical performance. If you were to experience *concern*, however, you would be more able to cope with the uncertainty of the situation while remaining mentally sharp and fully focussed. Although you may wish to feel confident and calm in the situations I've just described, the reality is that this would be highly unlikely if there's a lot at stake for you and you feel strongly about the outcome. However, if you aim at moving from *anxiety* to *concern* by using the strategies I'll teach you, you may eventually experience confidence and calm in stressful situations. It's also worth noting that unhelpful negative beliefs tend to emanate from rigid or extreme thinking styles, whereas helpful negative emotions flow from flexible and preferential thoughts and beliefs.

Themes

Themes describe certain common features that occur in challenging present or future situations and apply equally to helpful and unhelpful negative emotions. You will see within the emotions table that the theme for both *anxiety* and *concern* is 'threat or danger' (e.g. the risk of drying up when giving a major presentation). But the thoughts you are more prone to have and the way you are more likely to behave will differ depending on which type of emotion you experience.

Thoughts

If you experience an unhelpful negative emotion like *anxiety*, you will be more inclined to focus your attention on negative aspects of the situation and overestimate the chances of something bad happening to you. This is similar to the process of *emotional reasoning* that I described earlier in this chapter whereby your perspective becomes distorted and you interpret what is happening to you based on how you are feeling. This can lead to a downward spiral in dwindling self-confidence as even the slightest evidence of 'things going wrong' (noticing a stern face in the front row as you are about to present) will reinforce your negative beliefs about the situation. If you experience helpful negative emotions, on the other hand, your focus of attention is more likely to be positive, realistic and constructive.

Behaviour

If you experience helpful negative emotions, you are more likely to engage in constructive behaviours that will help you to deal with any challenges you may encounter on the way to achieving your goals. Conversely, unhelpful negative emotions incline you towards self-defeating behaviours that sabotage attempts to achieve your goals. It's important to note that *the best way to break free from an unhelpful emotional state is to think and act in a way that's consistent with a helpful emotion.* What I mean by this is that if you feel anxious in a given situation, instead of giving in to the desire to retreat physically or mentally, compel yourself to confront the threat head-on and deal with it in a constructive manner. Changing the way you act is an effective method for altering your emotional states, and the table provides you with a range of helpful behaviours you can adopt. It's also worth emphasising that if you feel a strong urge to act in a certain way, it's indicative that you are experiencing the emotion consistent with that behaviour even if you don't act on that particular impulse. For example, if you were having an argument and felt a strong urge to punch your boss, this would normally indicate that you are experiencing *anger* rather than *annoyance* even if you don't follow through with the action.

A quantitative model of negative emotions

The emotions table provides you with a *qualitative* method for evaluating your feelings in challenging situations and for moving towards a more helpful emotional state. Hopefully it will also provide you with a better understanding of your emotional reactions and help you to develop constructive behavioural strategies to deal with challenges. You can also use a simpler *quantitative* model for assessing your emotional reactions to challenging situations and for setting yourself constructive emotional goals by using *Likert scales*. Let's consider this approach with regards to the emotion *anxiety*.

No anxiety...Intense anxiety

0   1   2   3   4   5   6   7   8   9   10

If you experience apprehension when faced with a particular challenge, try to objectively assess the intensity of your feelings. You might find it helpful to ask yourself the following question:

> *On a scale of 0 to 10, where 0 is totally relaxed and 10 is the most intense anxiety I have ever experienced, what rating would I give for my feelings about this particular challenge? (e.g. attending the interview, giving the presentation)?*

This will enable you to establish a baseline for your current level of anxiety (or any other unhelpful negative emotion) and to set an *emotional goal* as part of your strategy for dealing with this particular challenge, namely reducing your current level of anxiety. Try to be realistic when setting this goal – aiming at '0 anxiety' if you feel very strongly about the outcome of the challenge will be of little use.

> *Given that I feel very strongly about achieving this particular goal (getting the job, giving a winning presentation), what would be a realistic reduction to aim for?*

Let's assume that you rated your current level of anxiety at 8 when contemplating the challenge and you considered reducing this number to 2 as a realistic emotional goal. The next thing you need to do is consider which cognitive and behavioural strategies you will need to put in place in order to achieve this reduction.

> *In this situation, what are the most helpful ways I can* think *and* act *to reduce my level of anxiety from 8 to 2?*

You can then use the emotions table as a resource to help you review constructive thoughts and behaviours associated with helpful negative emotions (in this case *concern* as opposed to *anxiety)* to help you develop your strategy. You can use this process for any unhelpful negative emotion.

Now that I've given you a theoretical overview of the ABC model, I'd like to introduce you to a more detailed version and explain how to use it to overcome challenges and achieve your goals.

The ABCDE model

The ABCDE model offers you a powerful tool that will help you to:

1   Define any thinking errors you may be making that create additional psychological barriers to achieving your goal.
2   Break down specific challenges into manageable steps using the ABCDE framework.

We covered the ABC components in detail earlier. The different segments of the model are included in the following breakdown.

'A' = activating event: Often referred to as *adversity* as the situation is challenging in some way. The activating event can be *external*, when something real (as opposed to imagined) that has happened to you in the past is happening right now or is a future event that you anticipate. 'A' can also be an *internal* event (taking place in your mind and/or body) including images, dreams, memories and bodily sensations. 'A' activates or *triggers* your thoughts and beliefs about the situation.

'B' = beliefs: Any cognitive processes that get triggered by the *activating event* at 'A'. These include immediate automatic thoughts or subjective meanings you might read into the situation. At a deeper level 'B' might include any strongly held beliefs or rules for living you may have (your personal principles) that get triggered by something about the situation.

'C' = consequences: Beliefs/thinking processes that get triggered by the *activating event* including your emotional, behavioural and physical reactions.

'D' = disputing: A very important part of the model that involves you in actively challenging any unhelpful thoughts or beliefs that you have uncovered that lead you to experience unhelpful emotional and physical *consequences* at 'C'.

'E' = new and effective: Thinking that will give you the emotional, behavioural and physical resources to deal with your challenge more effectively.

I will now provide you with detailed instructions on completing an ABCDE formulation for any future challenge you find yourself faced with. A blank version of the ABCDE model can be found at Appendix 2.

Constructing an ABCDE formulation

Stage 1: Describe concisely what you want to achieve in the 'What is your goal?' section. Try to make your goal specific, measurable, achievable, realistic and time-bound (i.e. SMART).

Stage 2: Identify the emotion you are feeling in response to a particular situation in the Consequences (C) section, point 1.

The reason for starting at 'C' is because, if the situation is challenging, you are describing the emotional barrier getting in the way of achieving your particular goal. For example, this could be *anxiety* at the prospect of attending a job interview or giving a presentation. You can refer back to the emotions table in the previous section to help you understand and identify your emotional reaction to the situation.

Stage 3: Describe how you acted (or felt like acting) in the Consequences (C) section, point 2.

This could include unhelpful behaviour that is driven by the emotion you are experiencing and have identified at point 1. So in the case of *anxiety*, this might include the tendency to *seek reassurance that the threat won't happen* (e.g. asking others to tell you that nothing bad will happen at your interview or presentation). You can refer to the 'Behaviour' section of the emotions table to help you clarify how you might typically act or feel like acting in challenging situations.

Stage 4: Describe what it was about the situation that triggered your feelings in the Activating Event (A) section.

As I've previously mentioned, the 'activating event' is some specific aspect of the general situation that *triggers* a chain reaction of unhelpful thoughts, emotions and behaviours. These triggers get activated in situations that happen in:

The present: while you're giving the presentation or attending the interview

The past: thinking back on how badly the presentation or interview went

The future: thinking about what may go wrong with the presentation or interview

Remember, these triggers can be *internal* as well as *external*. When you're under pressure, you may notice *physical sensations* such as increased heartbeat, rapid breathing and perspiration. These symptoms can also become activating events and trigger unhelpful thinking.

It's always helpful to pinpoint the most challenging aspect of the situation so that you can carry out an accurate assessment. Two helpful questions to ask yourself are:

• *What is it about this situation that disturbs me the most?*
• *If there's one thing I could change about the situation that would make it tolerable, what would it be?*

If you find it difficult to determine a specific aspect, another approach is to list everything that you find challenging or disturbing about the situation and then rank them in order of magnitude. If we take the example of giving a presentation this could include:

1   Drying up in front of the audience
2   Being asked awkward questions I haven't prepared for
3   The projector or laptop failing
4   Blushing, sweating or trembling
5   Dropping my notes

Having listed and ranked your concerns, you would be able to determine that the key **activating event** at 'A' is the prospect of drying up in front of the audience and is your target as part of the formulation.

Stage 5: Describe any unhelpful thoughts or beliefs you have about the situation in the Belief (B) section.

If we take the above example of giving a presentation, typical unhelpful thoughts could include:

'I'm bound to dry up in front of everyone'.

'If someone asks me an awkward question, I won't be able to answer it'.

'Something will probably go wrong with the equipment – it usually does!'

'I'll go bright red, start sweating and shaking – everyone will notice!'

'I'll drop my notes and won't be able to carry on'.

When you think about the situation, you may also experience *catastrophic images* as well as verbal thoughts. With regards to the presentation, you might *see* yourself getting flustered in front of the audience, go red and start visibly shaking. You could then imagine the audience looking on sternly as you humiliate yourself. Note any of these images in this section.

Step 6: Consider any thinking errors you are making about the situation and note them in the Dispute (D) section.

You may wish to refer back to the unhelpful patterns of thinking section in this chapter in order to help you identify self-sabotaging thoughts that will undermine your performance. Ask yourself the following questions:

'Am I focussing on the absolute worst thing that could happen but that's highly unlikely?' (catastrophising)

'Am I thinking in extreme, all-or-nothing terms?' (black-and-white thinking)

'Am I berating myself with terms such as "I *always* fail" or "I *never* do well"?' (over-generalisation)

'Am I making negative predictions about what is going to happen?' (fortune telling)

'Am I making negative interpretations about what other people are thinking about me?' (mind reading)

'Am I focussing on just the negative aspects of the situation without taking anything positive into account?' (mental filtering)

'Am I engaging in unhelpful, self-attacking thinking – calling myself a failure, for example?' (labelling)

'Am I being misled by my negative gut instincts about the situation without balanced rational thinking?' (emotional reasoning)

'Am I telling myself that I won't be able to bear the situation (e.g. nervousness during the presentation) when it's uncomfortable but tolerable and a price worth paying for the outcome?' (low frustration as opposed to high frustration tolerance)

Stage 7: Having gone through the disputing process at Step 6, note any helpful motivational thoughts in the Effective Thinking (E) section.

As part of this process, return to column B and enter comments under points 1–3 as follows:

Point 1: Describe a helpful alternative for each negative thought, belief or attitude previously recorded.

Point 2: Describe how you would prefer to feel about the situation (your emotional goal).

Point 3: Describe what constructive action you intend to take (your behavioural goals).

This step is vitally important as one of the key principles of CBT concerns *thinking* and *acting* in opposition to negative automatic thoughts and beliefs to turn the situation to your advantage.

Another useful series of questions you can ask yourself when feeling overwhelmed by a challenge is:

• 'What's the worst that can happen?'
• 'What's the *best* that can happen?'
• 'What's the most likely thing that will happen?'

This has the effect of *thought balancing*: imagining both extreme ends of the spectrum about the situation in order to pitch your expectations somewhere in the middle.

Stage 8: Develop a plan of attack.

This final stage pulls everything together as you describe the key actions you will take to meet your challenge head-on in Section 'E', 'Action Plan'.

Using cognitive counter-attacks to strengthen new effective thinking

Using the ABCDE model will help you to challenge unhelpful thoughts that arise when you face stressful situations on the way to achieving your personal goals. But even after you have developed *new effective thinking* at 'E' within the model, you may still have reservations about adopting a more positive outlook, without even knowing it, at an unconscious level. You know that thinking in this way would be psychologically more helpful but your feelings are not in alignment with your thoughts. This is because you have probably gained an *intellectual* insight with regards to your particular challenge but not an *emotional* insight. Let me explain this idea in a little more detail.

Albert Ellis (1963), the creator of REBT, made a distinction between the two types of insight that we gain when we realise that our cognitive and behavioural strategies in pursuit of our goals are defective. He observed that when we gain intellectual insight that we are thinking about our challenges in unhelpful, irrational ways and that we can think more constructively and rationally, this insight is merely a superficial acknowledgement. This type of epiphany is often described as an 'ah-ha' moment and we can feel a great deal of satisfaction from gaining this new understanding for perhaps the first time in our lives. But Ellis pointed out that it is at this very moment of realisation that we risk deluding ourselves that insight alone is enough to overcome any psychological barriers that we have battled against previously when pursuing our goals. For example, if you struggle with public speaking engagements, you may have suddenly realised that this difficulty is linked to the anxiety you felt when having to present in front of the class at school in your early childhood. However, gaining this understanding alone will not be enough to help you think and act more confidently when giving presentations in front of large groups. For that to happen, you will need to gain *emotional insight*.

Intellectual insight (the head)

↓

Emotional insight (the heart)

Essentially, you need to transfer your new helpful insight from your head to your heart so that you believe it at an emotional level. This means committing yourself to the hard work of *thinking* and *acting* consistently with your new effective outlook in stressful situations while battling with your old negative thoughts if they come back to haunt you. If you don't commit yourself wholeheartedly to this approach, you will merely learn *why* you fail in certain situations without being able to do anything constructive about it. This means being honest with yourself and accepting that there will inevitably be a price to pay for attaining your particular goal – perhaps experiencing some emotional and related physical discomfort (e.g. experiencing concern rather than anxiety). But growth rarely comes without some form of discomfort and is almost always worth paying the price.

A good way of strengthening your effective new thinking strategy and gaining *emotional insight* is to play the role of *devil's advocate* by both attacking and defending your new outlook. This will help strengthen your conviction and pre-empt any self-doubts that may occur when you're under pressure at a later stage. The important thing to emphasise is that you need to launch increasingly aggressive attacks on your effective new thinking style in order to strengthen it. This is similar to the practice of karate and other martial arts in which you are required to fight

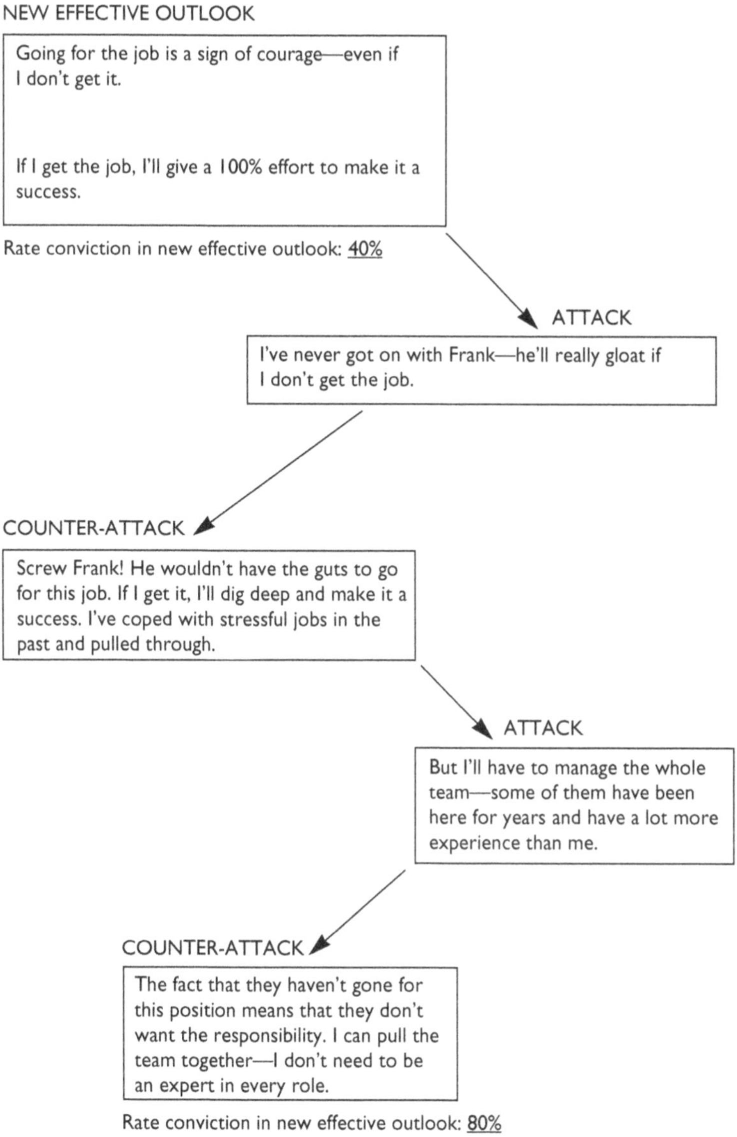

NEW EFFECTIVE OUTLOOK

> Going for the job is a sign of courage—even if I don't get it.
>
> If I get the job, I'll give a 100% effort to make it a success.

Rate conviction in new effective outlook: <u>40%</u>

ATTACK

> I've never got on with Frank—he'll really gloat if I don't get the job.

COUNTER-ATTACK

> Screw Frank! He wouldn't have the guts to go for this job. If I get it, I'll dig deep and make it a success. I've coped with stressful jobs in the past and pulled through.

ATTACK

> But I'll have to manage the whole team—some of them have been here for years and have a lot more experience than me.

COUNTER-ATTACK

> The fact that they haven't gone for this position means that they don't want the responsibility. I can pull the team together—I don't need to be an expert in every role.

Rate conviction in new effective outlook: <u>80%</u>

Figure 1.5 Colin's cognitive counter-attack worksheet.

increasingly capable opponents as you progress to black belt and beyond in order to increase your physical and psychological prowess. Let's look at how Colin used this approach to help him gain confidence in going for an internal promotion within his organisation.

Colin's challenge

Colin has been working for a number of years within his company as a relatively junior accountant and constantly feels frustrated at his lack of progression within the organisation. One day, quite unexpectedly, the financial controller hands in her notice as she has been head-hunted by a rival company. Colin has long coveted the role but is suddenly ambivalent about applying. Puzzled by his reaction to this longed-for opportunity, Colin carries out an ABCDE assessment and determines that he holds a number of unhelpful beliefs about the situation, namely that (a) colleagues will think he's a failure if he doesn't get the job; and (b) even if he got the job, he wouldn't be able to cope. Colin has used the ABCDE framework to dispute these negative beliefs and has formulated an effective new outlook. However, no matter how many times he repeats this to himself, Colin still doesn't feel a high level of conviction and decides submit his new outlook to the **cognitive counter-attacking process** (Figure 1.5).

Using the cognitive counter-attack worksheet

You can use the worksheet at Appendix 3 as a means of strengthening conviction in your new effective outlook and moving it from your head to your heart. This will stand you in good stead for when you practise this new thinking style in challenging situations on the way to achieving you goal. Just follow these instructions.

Stage 1: Record your new effective outlook in the top left-hand box and rate your current level of conviction in this statement on a scale of 0 to 100 per cent.

Stage 2: In the next box, describe any doubts you may have about your new effective outlook. Remember, be completely honest and attack your positive outlook with any reservations that you may have as energetically as possible. Better to raise these doubts now rather than experience them spontaneously when you engage with the challenge and are under pressure.

Stage 3: In the next box down, throw yourself into the counter-attack, demolishing any negative thoughts you have had that will undermine your confidence. Always make these responses consistent with your new effective outlook and avoid going off on different tangents.

Stage 4: Keep repeating stages 2 and 3 until you have counter-attacked every doubt, reservation and negative thought in relation to your new effective outlook. You may need to use several worksheets to completely neutralise any lingering reservations and fully strengthen your conviction. Make sure you conclude on a counter-attack so that every doubt is vanquished.

Stage 5: Once you have thoroughly exhausted any remaining doubts, re-rate your level of conviction in the effective new outlook on a scale of 0 to 100 per cent. If your level of conviction hasn't increased significantly, this may indicate that you still have reservations that haven't been addressed adequately. Close your eyes and tune in to how you are feeling *emotionally* when you rehearse your new effective outlook. If you notice some unease or dissonance, try to give words to this feeling as you may flush out a lingering doubt that still needs to be addressed.

It's worth noting that although this process is a paper and pencil exercise, like many of the tools on offer in this book, initial practice of these techniques in writing will eventually lead you to internalise these approaches so that they become automatic mental responses for countering unhelpful negative thinking in challenging situations.

In Chapter 2, and for the remainder of this book, we will build on the theory you have learned and apply it to one of the key areas for achieving success in your career: the formal job interview.

If you forget everything else I've taught you in this chapter, remember this:

1   We have 50,000 thoughts per day – not all of them are helpful.
2   Our thoughts actually change the physical structures of our brains – for better or worse.
3   Our thoughts, emotions, physiological responses and behavioural reactions interact in complex ways and are triggered by life challenges.
4   Unhelpful beliefs about ourselves often develop in childhood, but we can challenge them and change them.
5   We need to be guided by our emotions, not misled by them.
6   We have the power to change the way we think, feel and act in response to future, present and past situations.

Note

1   According to the National Science Foundation.

References

Beck, J. S. (2011). *Cognitive behaviour therapy: basics and beyond.* Guilford Press.

Ellis, A. (1963). Toward a more precise definition of 'emotional' and 'intellectual' insight. *Psychological Reports*, 23, 538–40.

Fox, E. (2012). *Rainy brain, sunny brain.* Basic Books.

Frankl, V. (1984). *Man's search for meaning.* Washington Square Press

Korzybski, A. (1995). *Science and sanity: an introduction to non-Aristotelian systems and general semantics.* Institute of General Semantics

Maguire, E., Gadian, D., Johnsrude, I., Good, C., Ashburner, J., Frackowiak, R. and Frith, C. (2000). Navigation related structural change in the hippocampi of taxi drivers. *Proceedings of the National Academy of Sciences*, 97(8), 4398–4403.

Mandela, N. (1995). *The Long Walk to Freedom.* Macdonald Purnell.

Neenan, M. (2009). *Developing resilience: a cognitive-behavioural approach.* Routledge.

Neenan, M. and Dryden, W. (2011). *Rational emotive behaviour therapy in a nutshell.* SAGE.

Seligman, M. E. P. (2002). *Authentic happiness.* Free Press.

Young, J. E. and Klosko, J. S. (1994). *Reinventing your life.* Plume.

Chapter 2

Using cognitive and behavioural approaches to succeed at interview

Hopefully you will have gained a reasonable understanding of CBT theory from Chapter 1 and you can refer back to its foundation models as you progress through this book and build on your skills and knowledge. In this chapter, I will help you apply what you have learned so far to one of the most important challenges for achieving a successful career, namely succeeding at formal interviews. I will teach you various motivational and confidence building strategies including the use of visualisation techniques. But before we go any further, I want to teach you how to carry out a formulation within the context of a forthcoming interview using either the ABC or life challenges model that we encountered in Chapter 1.

Developing a formulation of the forthcoming interview

Before you engage in any psychological preparation for the interview, you need to do as much practical preparation as possible within the time available to you. Essential tasks you need to cover include:

*   Researching the company thoroughly and getting a sense of its culture, mission and core values
*   Studying the job and person specification and drafting a list of questions that the interviewers may ask to determine whether you meet the requirements of the position
*   Drafting answers to the questions you've anticipated and considering the possibility of role plays and what the interviewers may focus on
*   Deciding how you will travel to the venue and calculating enough time with a margin of error in case of delays

- Choosing clothing for the interview that will make you feel confident in terms of self-presentation and also conform with the company's house style

All of the above tasks are within your *external* range of control. Once you have covered these, the next step is to take charge of your *internal* range of control by identifying any mental or emotional obstacles that lie in your way and developing an effective psychological strategy. As you have seen in Chapter 1, carrying out an ABC formulation on challenging situations enables you to determine any potential thinking errors you may engage in and define the emotional and behavioural consequences. Let's look at a typical example of an ABC formulation for one of my clients, Jonathan, who had applied for a position as a senior recruitment consultant in a central London firm specialising in placing accountants into work.

Steve: Last time we met you'd applied for this job but you didn't think you had much chance of getting an interview because of the amount of competition for these positions.

Jonathan: That's right. Now I've got an interview, I *really* want the job but I don't think I stand much of a chance.

Steve: Why's that?

Jonathan: It's a high pressure sales position, very well-paid. But I know from a friend who'd previously applied that the interview panel deliberately test your reaction to stress – the process is very adversarial.

Steve: What makes you think you can't cope with that level of pressure at interview?

Jonathan: Whenever I get anxious, I can feel my face becoming flushed and I know they will *see* my anxiety. They'll know that I can't handle stressful situations and reject me.

Steve: I know that you've spent a lot of time researching the company and anticipating the kind of questions you're likely to receive. How do you feel about doing some psychological preparation?

Jonathan: I can't think of anything else that would help right now.

Steve: OK. I'd like to map this out on the flip chart so that we can get a better understanding of your thinking processes and how they're impacting on your mood. We know that the situation you find daunting is the panel interview; let's put that on the board.

Situation:

High pressure panel interview

Steve: When you think about the interview that's coming up, you get anxious. What's driving that anxiety? If you had to be specific, what's the worst thing about that situation?

Jonathan: As I said, it's the possibility that I'll feel my face flushing when I get stressed.

Steve: Ok, let's put that on the flip chart.

Situation:

High pressure panel interview

'**A**' = The possibility of feeling my face flush during the interview

Steve: If that were to happened during the interview, what would you think?

Jonathan: That the panel can *see* I'm anxious and think that can't cope with pressure.

Steve: So if we write that thought at 'B', it looks like this:

Situation:

High pressure panel interview

'**A**' = The possibility of feeling my face flush during the interview

'**B**' = The panel will see that I'm anxious and think that I can't cope with pressure

Steve: And if that thought occurs to you during the interview, how do you think you'll feel?

Jonathan: At that point I'll feel even more anxious because I'd know they were aware of my nerves.

Steve: How will you know you're anxious – what changes will you notice in your body?

Jonathan: When this sort of thing happens, my heart starts to beat faster and I become slightly light headed.

Steve: What sort of an impact will all of this have on your performance during the interview?

Jonathan: I reckon it'll all start to fall apart. I'll become so self-conscious that I won't be able to recover my concentration and I'll lose track of the questions.

Steve: So, a lot of unhelpful consequences start to happen.

Situation:

High pressure panel interview

'**A**' = The possibility of feeling my face flush during the interview

'**B**' = The panel will see that I'm anxious and think that I can't cope with pressure

'**C**' = *Emotional:* Increased anxiety; *Physical:* increased heartbeat, light-headedness; *Behavioural:* increased self-consciousness, poor concentration, impaired performance

Steve:	Now I want you to really focus on the formulation that we've just completed. Where do you think the biggest problem is? Is it at 'A', 'B' or 'C'?
Jonathan:	It's definitely at A – the situation and the possibility that my face might start to flush.
Steve:	But that's not going to go away. Assuming you want to put yourself forward for this job, you can't change the situation and there will always be a chance of your face feeling flushed.
Jonathan:	OK, it's 'C'. If I didn't get such a strong reaction, I could perform better at the interview.
Steve:	I know it doesn't seem immediately apparent, but the situation at 'A' isn't leading to the consequences you're getting at 'C'. The problem lies in the way you're thinking at 'B'.
Jonathan:	But it's true – if my face flushes, they'll think I'm weak.
Steve:	How do you know that? You're falling into a very common trap that people experience when they get stressed at interviews: you're *mind reading.* The interview panel could be thinking a number of other things if they notice you flushing slightly – that you're hot, that you're passionate about what you're saying. The point is that you've no accurate way of knowing what they're thinking at any stage in the interview. How do you even know it's noticeable when your face feels flushed?
Jonathan:	It *feels* very noticeable.
Steve:	That's because you've already told yourself that it's the worst thing that could happen so when you notice any sensations, you focus on them intensively. But the critical question is this: Will thinking this way help you perform well at the interview?
Jonathan:	Definitely not. I hadn't considered what a dramatic impact my thoughts can have on my feelings and behaviour.

Steve: So how can you change your thinking at 'B' to empower you rather than obstruct you at the interview?

Jonathan: I suppose I could tell myself that even if I flush, they won't know if I'm feeling nervous. If I act confidently, it could be a sign of my enthusiasm.

Steve: That's right. So let's re-work the model using your new insight.

Situation:
High pressure panel interview

'A' = The possibility of feeling my face flush during the interview

'B' = Even if my face flushes, they won't know it's anxiety – it could be a sign of enthusiasm

'C' = *Emotional:* Increased confidence; *Physical:* high energy but calm; *Behavioural:* confident self-presentation, focussed attention

Steve: You mentioned that you didn't realise how big an impact your thoughts can have on your feelings and actions. Has this approach helped you to gain that insight?

Jonathan: Definitely. Breaking the problem down into different parts has helped me to gain a more objective perspective on the situation – it doesn't seem so overwhelming.

Steve: Would you like me to teach you the model in a little more detail so that you can use it in other challenging situations?

Jonathan: I'd appreciate that.

As you may have realised, we could also use the life challenges model to carry out a formulation of Jonathan's forthcoming interview, which would look like Figure 2.1.

Both models have their own distinct advantages and it's largely a matter of preference in terms of using them to carry out formulations of challenging situations like interviews. The life challenges model will enable you to see clearly the interplay between your thoughts, feelings, physiological responses and behavioural reactions and help you to consider strategies for breaking out of any negative cycles. The ABC model helpfully illustrates the causality that occurs when we think in an unhelpful way about challenging situations and the chain reaction of emotional, physiological and behavioural consequences. Of the two models, it provides a more comprehensive methodology for challenging unhelpful thoughts and developing constructive strategies.

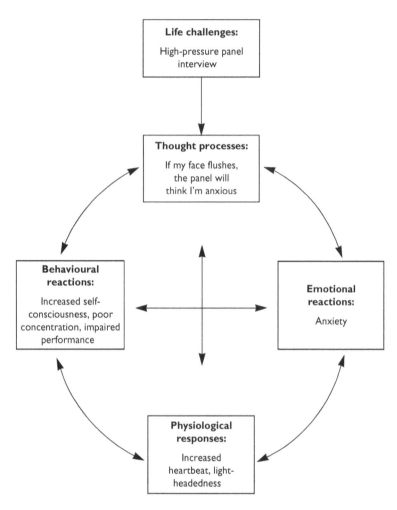

Figure 2.1 Jonathan's life challenges formulation.

Whichever model you chose, it's really important for you to put into practice the new constructive thoughts and behaviours that you have developed as part of your formulation. This may feel a little strange at first, even though you have worked hard to strengthen conviction in your new effective outlook by using the *cognitive counter-attacking* process described in Chapter 1. For example, Jonathan may agree that it's a good idea for him to act confidently at the interview and tell himself that even if his face flushes, it could be interpreted as a sign of enthusiasm rather than anxiety. But he also needs to follow through by acting and thinking confidently at the interview. We will now consider the role of anxiety in challenging situations and explore a number of methods you can use to counter its effects.

Managing anxiety

Most of us experience interviews as stressful situations, both in anticipation of and during the event. This is understandable, as you're facing a competitive situation and there's a lot a stake – not least your self-esteem if you don't succeed. Unless you're a Buddhist monk, some anxiety at interviews is inevitable. The problem for many people is that they absolutely *hate* feeling anxious and, because it's such a visceral experience, they perceive it as a threat and an indication that they will not be able to cope with the challenging situation. That's why I want to help you understand what happens in your mind and body when you feel anxious, and why this emotion and its physical consequences are actually helpful, although it often feels uncomfortable.

Where did anxiety come from?

Evolutionary theorists from Charles Darwin in *The origin of the species* (2011) to Richard Dawkins in *The selfish gene* (2006) have suggested that what we perceive to be negative emotions, such as anxiety and aggression, have a survival utility and were passed on to us by our ancient ancestors through natural selection. You've probably heard of the 'fight or flight' response first described by American physiologist Walter Canon (1920). According to this notion, when our ancient ancestors encountered a sudden threat (a large animal or another homo sapiens) he had a split second to decide whether to attack or run away. Depending on his instinct, this would trigger *anxiety* or *aggression* with very similar physical consequences (which is why the two emotions are very closely linked). Our ancestors who responded most effectively were more likely to survive, find a mate (because they were better at gathering resources), procreate and pass on their aggressive and anxious genes to successive generations—in some respects it's very much like modern corporate life.

These emergency responses were driven by the most ancient part of our brain – the brainstem or 'reptilian brain' controlling physical levels of arousal. Our brains have developed over millions of years, evolving outward from the brainstem to the limbic regions, which enable us to evaluate situations, to the neocortex and lastly the prefrontal cortex, which enables us to use language, engage in abstract thinking and have a sense of our own unique identity. In *Mindsight* (2013), professor of psychiatry Daniel Siegel uses a hand model of the brain to illustrate its physical evolution and the way in which the brainstem, limbic area and cortex interconnect. Try it yourself: Make a fist with your right hand and tuck your thumb under your fingers. Now raise your fist so that your fingers and palm are facing you. The top of your fingers represent the *cerebral cortex* and the tips of your fingers represent the *prefrontal cortex*. Finally, the place where your palm and wrist interconnect represents the *brainstem* linking to the *spinal cord* represented by your wrist.

The physical consequences of anxiety

Just like our ancient ancestors, when we perceive a threat, our limbic brain, controlling emotions and physiological responses, becomes activated and triggers our autonomic nervous system, specifically the *sympathetic nervous system* responsible for the 'fight or flight' reaction. This in turn leads to a number of physiological consequences that can seem threatening but, on closer examination, offer a finely tuned response marshalling the body's resources to deal with challenges.

Dry mouth: This indicates that our digestion has slowed down or ceased so that it's not using energy needed elsewhere.

Rapid breathing: Our lungs are providing the blood with more oxygen for energy.

Increased blood pressure: More blood is pumped around the body, carrying oxygen.

Indigestion/nausea: Digestion slows or ceases so that it doesn't divert energy.

Sweating: The body gets rid of heat.

Tense shoulders/neck/back: Large muscles contract, ready for action.

Blurred vision/red mist: Pupils dilate to help us focus all our attention where needed.

Headache/dizziness: An indication that the brain is producing adrenaline for energy.

Even some of the most disconcerting physical symptoms of anxiety have a helpful utility in an emergency. Have you ever observed anyone turning pale when anxious? This indicates that blood drains away from their peripheral circulation and is diverted to major limbs such as the arms and legs for action. It also means that if they get cut, they'll bleed less. When you feel nervous and want to go to the toilet – how's that helpful? It means that after the call of nature you'd be carrying less weight if you have to run away.

So, anxiety is meant to help us deal with emergencies and other challenges but what we want is a *proportionate response* to the situation in hand. A job interview is not an emergency so you don't need an all-out primal response. However, some moderate anxiety can be very helpful in providing you with an optimum amount of adrenaline to sharpen your mental responses. Think of it like driving a car and using the accelerator. Occasionally you need a burst of power to get you out of trouble but if you keep your foot on the pedal for too long, you'll burn out the engine. How do you obtain that balance? Let's have a look at some different strategies.

Riding the elephant

In *The happiness hypothesis* (2006), Jonathan Haidt makes the point that the ancient, instinctive brainstem and limbic areas comprise a much greater proportion of our brains than the later developed rational prefrontal cortex and he uses the metaphor of the *elephant and the rider*. When we're thinking rationally, our prefrontal cortex 'rider' has control over the potentially unruly emotional responses of the limbic/brainstem 'elephant'. But occasionally when we become emotionally aroused, the relationship changes and the elephant runs away with the rider. In extreme examples this response can leave you completely paralysed with fear; Daniel Goleman (1996) refers to this as 'emotional hijacking'. How do you regain control when your anxiety is increasing and your capacity for thinking clearly is compromised? Daniel Siegel (2013) suggests a process called 'name it to tame it'. By actually saying to yourself (not necessarily out loud), 'I'm feeling slightly anxious about the interview but that's perfectly normal', you activate the language centres located in the left prefrontal cortex and this in turn has a calming effect on the emotional areas of the brain. Neuropsychologists use magnetic resonance imaging (MRI) scans to examine brain activity and can see how the rider regains control of the elephant. We've already used the ABC model to help you determine if you're falling into any negative thinking patterns prior to the interview and we've replaced these with more balanced, helpful thoughts. Every time you practice these thoughts, you will activate your rational left prefrontal cortex and regain control of the elephant.

Accepting anxiety – don't fight the elephant

If you feel nervous at the prospect of attending an interview, you need to acknowledge these feelings – you can even say 'hello' to your nerves. Struggling against feelings of nervousness or trying to supress them will only prove counterproductive. While we're on the subject of elephants, if I told you to try as hard as possible not to think of a pink elephant for one minute, chances are that the image would keep popping into your mind (try it). The term used for this response in psychology is *paradoxical rebound*. Essentially, the more we try to supress thoughts and feelings, the likelier we are to experience them even more intensely. A clinical example of this is patients I've worked with who suffer from obsessive compulsive disorder (OCD) and who experience intrusive thoughts. This includes religious practitioners who have experienced an arbitrary thought that they may one day swear in church. Understandably, they make every effort to control their cognitive processes, but this usually results in an even greater number of unbidden blasphemous thoughts. A more effective strategy than thought or feeling suppression is to accept the fact that *nervousness is normal* before or during an interview and that the associated physical sensations are not a sign of losing control but a gathering of resources that will help you sharpen your performance (the adrenaline will enable you to react more quickly to challenging questions). As I've mentioned previously, these physical symptoms of nervousness are *internal events* and can trigger negative thoughts that increase anxiety if you pay too much attention to them. Having 'gone inside' and acknowledged these symptoms, it's time now to focus your attention on the external environment.

Taking control of your attention

As I mentioned, if you continue to pay undue attention to physical symptoms of anxiety you risk distracting yourself from the task in hand and this may inhibit your performance during the interview. We frequently use the term 'self-conscious' without thinking of its deeper meaning. It's perfectly understandable that you may experience some performance anxiety if you have an interviewer or a panel watching you closely. But if you focus exclusively on how you are feeling and begin monitoring your performance during the interview, you're more likely to get into the vicious cycle we've seen previously. An effective way of managing your anxiety during interviews (and any other interpersonal interactions) is to refocus attention away from yourself, which will require you to develop the skill of *task concentration*. Your aim during the interview should be to direct approximately 80 per cent of your attention on the *task* and *environment*, as you can see in Figure 2.2 below.

As I mentioned previously, trying to deny or suppress feelings of nervousness before the interview will be counterproductive; it's more helpful to 'go inside' and acknowledge them. But after checking in, focussing on yourself and reminding yourself that 'nervousness is normal', you then need to refocus your attention on your immediate environment and

Figure 2.2 Focus of attention pie chart.

Reproduced from Sheward and Branch (2012), *Motivational Career Counselling and Coaching: Cognitive and behavioural approaches*, SAGE.

the task in hand. *Task concentration* is a useful skill and can be used in a variety of high pressure situations in addition to interviews (e.g. public speaking) where the risk of becoming self-conscious is increased – but it requires practice.

Chances are that you already manage to filter out a wide range of distractions and focus your attention in a variety of situations without even being aware of it. For example:

• Sitting in a restaurant or a bar engrossed in conversation with a friend. There may be a great deal of background noise but you manage to filter it out because you're intent on hearing what your friend has to tell you.
• Having a conversation on your mobile in a busy environment you become far less aware of what's going on around you.
• Reading an engrossing book on a train you ignore the sound of conversations going on around you and other ambient noise.
• Working out in the gym listening to energetic music or watching TV distracts you from feelings of physical fatigue or aching limbs.
• A tight deadline is looming, so you focus almost 100 per cent of your attention on the task and are less distracted by your work environment.

You can probably think of other examples, but the key point is that you *can* focus your attention when you feel motivated – that's usually because there's a reward (enjoying a novel, talking to a friend) or punishment (a reprimand from the boss if you miss the deadline) that's driving your behaviour. I want to encourage you to practice task concentration *at will* so that when you're faced with a challenging situation, like an interview or public speaking event, you'll be able to focus you attention away from feelings of self-consciousness and anxiety and onto the task in hand for optimal performance. Try the following exercise.

Choose a situation that isn't too challenging: Perhaps you're seeing friends or engaging in a social event where you will be fairly relaxed. Alternatively, choose a routine meeting at work where you feel confident.

Start by focussing on yourself: Deliberately 'go inside' and tune into how you're feeling emotionally (bored, engaged), notice any thoughts you may have about the interaction and how you view yourself in the situation (how am I coming across, how do I appear to others?).

Now focus on the environment: While you're interacting with your friends or colleagues, gradually focus your attention on what you can see, hear and smell (hopefully this will be a pleasant experience). Tune into any physical sensations associated with the external environment – the feeling of the chair your sitting in, resting your hand on the table, drinking water or some beverage.

Shift your attention to the task in hand: Really concentrate on the conversation you're having with friends or colleagues. Focus closely on facial expressions, mannerisms, gestures and tone of voice and immerse yourself in the flow of the conversation.

Review your experience after the event: What did it feel like when you deliberately moved your attention away from yourself and onto the environment and then the task? Were there any difficulties that you experienced when trying to manage your focus of attention, and how could you overcome these next time?

Increase the challenge: In order to strengthen your skill in *task concentration*, you need to practice focussing your attention away from yourself and onto the environment and the main task in increasingly challenging situations. Choose a situation that takes you out of your comfort zone but that is not overwhelming. This could include a situation at work in which you don't feel completely confident or where there are more distractions (trying to read a complicated document in a crowded, noisy place).

Practising *task concentration* in increasingly challenging situations will strengthen control over your attention so that when the pressure is on during an interview, you can cut through any negative thoughts and physical sensations of anxiety and turn your focus onto performing the task with minimum internal distraction. As I mentioned, this skill can be used in many high pressure situations such as public speaking, so it's well worth practising. We'll look at increasing your focus of attention in more detail later in Chapter 5.

Relax and focus on the breath

Earlier on in this chapter I mentioned that when we become anxious our *sympathetic nervous system* is activated and it can in turn trigger our 'fight or flight' response. If this response is proportionate to the challenge, the nervous energy we derive (through increased adrenaline) may be helpful – like putting our foot down on the accelerator. If the response is excessive and anxiety threatens to overwhelm us and undermine our performance, it's helpful to apply the brake, and this is where the *parasympathetic nervous system* proves useful. The *parasympathetic nervous system*, or PNS, initiates 'rest and digest' processes in our bodies (reduced heart rate, lower pulse rate, digestion after eating) and acts as a calming counterbalance to the exciting but eventually exhausting *sympathetic nervous system*. And the good news is that the PNS can be directly stimulated by breathing – particularly deep breathing. The most effective way of breathing deeply to initiate this soothing process is abdominal or *diaphragmatic breathing*.

The diaphragm is a large muscle located between the chest and stomach cavities; expanding and contracting this muscle can enhance deep breathing as the majority of people engage in shallow thoracic or 'chest breathing' using the intercostal muscles rather than the diaphragm. The importance of this form of breathing is stressed in many meditative practices and martial arts as it is deemed fundamental to the flow of energy. If you haven't practised this approach before, you might like to try the following exercise:

1   Find somewhere quiet and sit comfortably – straighten your back if this does not cause you any discomfort.
2   Now place one hand on your stomach and breathe out slowly while contracting your abdominal muscles gently – don't strain.
3   Just follow the natural rhythm of your breath and notice how your hand rises and falls as you inhale and exhale. Focus on inhaling slowly through your nostrils, tracing your breath through your chest and down to your stomach and then gently exhaling.
4   Notice the subtle, soothing sensation of breathing this way – the slight coolness of the breath entering your nostrils as you inhale and its warmth as you exhale.
5   Once you have fallen into a natural rhythm of breathing deeply, you may wish to recite a relaxing word in your mind each time you breathe out, 'c-a-l-m' for example. Many people find it helpful to visualise the breath slowly entering and leaving their body and enhance this image by imbuing the breath with a soothing, energy giving colour of your choice.
6   If any agitating thoughts about the interview occur to you, don't try to block them out. Just note them and let them drift away as you bring your attention back to your soothing breathing.

There are many ways in which you can practice this technique. If you notice yourself feeling anxious in the days leading up to the interview, try spending 5–10 minutes each day practising your deep breathing and notice its soothing effect. You can also practice this technique anywhere (including when you're waiting to go into the interview) by bringing your attention back to your breath and reciting a word that evokes a sense of calm when you exhale.

As with any other skill, frequent practice will be rewarded. Eventually you will reach a point where you breathe diaphragmatically all the time without conscious effort and you will, hopefully, derive the benefits of feeling calmer and more energised.

Using visualisation techniques to prepare for interviews

Formal interviews are future events and, according to CBT theory, our subjective predictions about what may happen can act as a trigger for negative thoughts leading to feelings of anxiety and unhelpful physical symptoms (sweating, increased heartbeat) which may have an adverse influence on the way we behave during the interview. One of the main reasons as to why we *make* ourselves anxious before an interview and other challenging future events (engaging in a difficult negotiation, for example) is because they are *unfamiliar*. Even if you do everything you can to prepare thoroughly, it's impossible to predict the outcome with any certainty. Using visualisation techniques will help you to reduce some of the uncertainty that you may feel about what lays ahead by helping you to mentally rehearse attending the interview. Using this approach will help you to psychologically 'ease into' the interview on the day because your mental rehearsal will have reduced the sense of it being an unfamiliar event. But why is imagery such a powerful tool?

Many evolutionary psychologists have suggested that we, as human beings, have developed a unique capacity to visualise future events and recall past events – an ability that even the most intelligent animals are incapable of. Their theory is that our primitive hunter-gatherer ancestors survived because they were able to recall places that offered the best hunting opportunities and visualise (or plan) visiting these locations in future. Our ancestors' ability to visualise is also reckoned to have aided them in crafting the first agricultural tools and in constructing the first buildings and temples. Today's leading architects still need to have a vision of the building they wish to create before engaging in the first steps of project planning.

Thus, using imagery is something we do instinctively as human beings and it is a strategy that has been passed on from our ancient ancestors through successive generations because it has helped us survive and flourish as a species. These days imagery is used widely within CBT to help clients overcome traumatic events (Hackmann, Bennett-Levy and Holmes, 2011) and in sports psychology to improve athletes' performance (Cumming and Ramsey, 2008; Jones and Stuth, 1997). Imagery is also used by many leading professionals (politicians, chief executives) in high pressure situations to optimise their performance. The reason these techniques are so powerful is that, at a certain level, our brains don't differentiate between something that we imagine (or create within our minds) and something that is actually taking place before us. All of this may sound rather bizarre or abstract, so I'd like you to keep an open mind and try the following exercise.

Exercise

I'd like you to close your eyes and sit in a comfortable but upright position. Imagine that in front of you there is a small table about waist height. In the centre of the table there is a light brown wooden chopping board and on top of this there is a large yellow lemon and a small silver knife.

Concentrate on the appearance of the lemon and notice how bright its yellow skin is and how its shiny surface reflects the light slightly.

Now pick up the lemon and feel its smooth, waxy skin between your fingertips. You might also notice the slight indentations and how it is firm but pliable when you squeeze it.

Place the lemon on the board and take the small silver knife in your hand. Now cut the lemon in half and listen for the hiss of juice escaping and the chopping sound when the blade makes contact with the wooden board.

Raise the lemon until it is just beneath your nose. Now slowly inhale the sharp, tangy smell and linger on the freshness of its fragrance.

Finally, bite into the flesh of the lemon and taste the sharp bitterness as its juices flow over your tongue and into your mouth. Notice the moist, pulpy texture of the lemon in your mouth.

What did you notice when you tried the exercise? You may have noticed that in addition to visualising the lemon, I also asked you to feel its skin, listen to the sound of the knife cutting through the lemon, smell its fragrance and finally taste its juice. Essentially, I was encouraging you to engage all five of your senses in creating an imagined experience, although I have described this approach under the heading of 'visualisation techniques'. This is very important as not everyone has a strong visual sense. You may have noticed that the images weren't particularly distinct but one or more of the other senses were. If you became immersed in the exercise you may have also noticed an increased amount of saliva in your mouth (most people do when I use this exercise in a group). What this indicates is that:

> Something you imagine can actually bring about a physical change in your body.

The mind actually has the power to do this either voluntarily or involuntarily. Let me explain this in a little more detail. You may have read accounts of combat veterans or accident victims suffering from symptoms of post-traumatic stress disorder (PTSD) in which they experience flashbacks following on from a traumatic incident, although it may have taken place years in the past. When these traumatic memories are triggered, it feels to these individuals as though they are actually re-experiencing the event *right now* when, in actual fact, their minds are re-creating a terrifying virtual experience which, as a consequence, brings about physical changes in their bodies. They may sweat, vomit, experience rapid heartbeat and even display marks on their skin (trauma therapists often say in reference to this that 'the body remembers'). This is a particularly dramatic illustration of the way in which imagined experience can effect physical change. More common examples include salivating when thinking about eating your favourite food or becoming physically aroused when engaging in erotic thoughts. The point is, you can harness the power of your mind to create a positive 'virtual experience' and I want to help you to do this by rehearsing attending your next interview 'in your mind'.

Mentally rehearsing the interview: exercise 1

Step 1: practical preparation

No amount of positive visualisation will help you with the interview unless you have devoted enough time to basic practical preparation and I would urge you to attend to the essential issues outlined at the beginning of this chapter. Your investment in practical preparation will be rewarded with increased confidence on the day of the interview. If you have the opportunity, try to enlist the help of a friend and carry out a role play of the interview so that you get the chance to answer anticipated questions in a spontaneous manner.

Once you've done everything within your control to prepare for the practical aspects of the interview, it's time to move on to psychological preparation through visualisation techniques.

Step 2: create a visual representation of the interview

Try to visit the venue where the interview is due to take place if possible. From a practical point of view, this will help you to plan the journey with greater accuracy but, more importantly, it will enable you to construct a visual representation of the venue to assist with your 'virtual reality' rehearsal of the interview. If you're not able to visit the venue, try to obtain a visual image of it by visiting the company website. It will also help you greatly if you can obtain images of the interviewer(s) so that they seem familiar to you when you meet them for the first time. In essence, do whatever you can to build up a visual representation of the interview, drawing on any knowledge and materials you have about the venue and staff involved. Even if it's not an accurate representation, you can still 'teach your mind' that the situation is familiar and therefore does not pose a threat due to its uncertainty.

Step 3: find somewhere quiet to practice your virtual interview experience

Try to find a calm, relaxing environment where you won't be disturbed by noise or interruptions. Wear loose clothing and sit in a comfortable but upright position. For maximum focus, it is recommended that you carry out the exercise with your eyes shut. If you regularly practice some form of meditation, you may wish to begin your rehearsal by clearing your mind before you begin the virtual interview experience. Alternatively, you can practice the relaxation breathing technique described earlier in this chapter.

Step 4: immerse yourself in the virtual interview experience

As I mentioned previously, it's important to engage all five of your senses in the virtual interview to make the experience as vivid as possible. Don't be discouraged if some of your senses seem less defined than others during this exercise. The process is similar to responses to different learning styles. Some individuals respond better to visual and aural stimuli (lectures, presentations), whereas others incline towards a kinaesthetic approach (hands on, practical).

Sight: You need to be fully associated with the situation. This means that you see the interview as it takes place through your eyes rather than watch yourself in a detached manner. This is very important in ensuring that you feel as though the experience is actually taking place. Look around as you approach the venue – slow things down. Focus on colours and shapes – are they vivid or subdued? Is it a bright day or cloudy?

Sound: As you look around, start to focus on any sounds that become apparent, such as the noise of the traffic, the receptionist addressing you as you enter the building, people passing by or the sound of the working environment. Try to notice where the sounds are coming from.

Smell: You may notice some pleasant fragrances, for example, the smell of flowers in the reception area, the aroma of freshly brewed coffee drifting in from nearby offices or a canteen.

Taste: As you sit waiting for the interview to take place, you may find it calming to sip a warm cup of tea or coffee or a cool glass of water – whatever you prefer. Notice the pleasant taste and the soothing temperature.

Touch: Tune into the physical aspects of the experience before you enter the venue. Notice the temperature, perhaps the sunshine or a pleasant breeze and your footsteps on the pavement. As you eventually enter the room where the interview will take place, feel yourself confidently shaking hands with the interviewer. As you sit in the chair, pay attention to feeling comfortable, solid and grounded sitting in the chair waiting for the interview to commence.

Step 5: Focus on your breathing and feeling calm

At this point, it may be helpful to focus on your breathing to anchor yourself by calming your mind and body. Notice the warm sensation of the breath entering your nostrils and then the gentle rhythm of breathing all the way down to your stomach and exhaling. Concentrate on the soothing sensations this engenders and feel them spread throughout your body.

Step 6: Nervousness is normal

If you begin to feel nervous at any stage of your virtual interview, just accept it as a normal part of the experience and bring your focus back to answering the questions in a confident manner. Don't mistake the feeling as a danger signal that things are going wrong and try to force it away;

rather, welcome the sensation as signifying an increase in adrenaline that will sharpen your mental reflexes and heighten performance.

Step 7: Practice makes perfect

If you were about to make a major presentation, you would be advised to rehearse it as many times as possible before the actual event. In the same way, the more you practise your virtual interview, the more familiar the scenario will seem to you and the greater your confidence on the day.

Practising the above approach will help you to tolerate moderate feelings of nervousness that may arise when you attend the interview. The following visualisation technique has a slightly different emphasis as it helps you to identify any self-defeating thoughts that may arise before or during the interview and develop strategies for countering them. The technique derives from rational emotive behaviour therapy (REBT), one of the earliest forms of CBT created by Albert Ellis. REBT places an emphasis on challenging negative thinking with a more balanced, rational outlook.

Mentally rehearsing the interview: exercise 2

Step 1: As with the previous exercise, find a quiet place, close your eyes and immerse yourself by tuning into the interview process through your five senses to make the experience as vivid as possible.

Step 2: Fast forward to the beginning of the interview and pay particular attention to any physical sensations that may arise. Do you notice any increase in heartbeat, irregular breathing, perspiration, muscular tension or any other physical symptoms of anxiety?

Step 3: Now notice any unhelpful thoughts that occur to you as the interview is taking place. Pay particular attention to any self-defeating thoughts that have been triggered by feelings of anxiety.

Step 4: Now imagine yourself managing to deal effectively with any feelings of anxiety that have arisen during the interview. If you have noticed physical symptoms of anxiety, acknowledge them as a normal response to a challenging situation and tell yourself that they are slightly uncomfortable but not dangerous. Feel yourself breathe slowly and evenly and notice feeling calm and grounded in your seat. Feel the tension ebb away and move your focus of attention away from any physical sensations and back to the interview process.

Step 5: Attack any negative thoughts the moment they arise with powerful counter-statements. Tell the negative voice in your head to shut up because you're doing just fine and you're not going to pay any attention to a few butterflies.

Step 6: Imagine yourself performing well at the interview, answering each question with confidence and feeling energy course through your body. See and hear the interviewers responding positively and end the session thinking that you have given your best performance.

Step 7: After you have completed the whole exercise, make a careful note of any strategies that you used spontaneously to combat any negative thoughts that arose during the interview and deal with physical sensations of anxiety. You can add these additional resources to your repertoire of skills and knowledge for attending the interview. As with the previous exercise, continued practice is highly recommended to strengthen your resilience in the face of pressure on the day.

You may ask yourself, "What if I do all this mental preparation and the interview turns out to be a nightmare and I don't get the job?" Unfortunately, a negative outcome may be completely beyond your control in spite of diligent practical and psychological preparation (the interviewers may be inexperienced, biased or threatened by you because of the skills and knowledge you offer). The important thing to stress is that *if you imagine a negative outcome, you are more likely to fail.* Picturing yourself doing badly at the interview will trigger negative thinking leading to increased anxiety, both of which will inhibit your performance. Conversely, neuroscience, cognitive science and sports psychology research suggests that positive imagery interventions have a powerful motivational effect and will equip you with the appropriate resources you need to complete the task successfully (Hackmann, Bennett-Levy and Holmes, 2011). Essentially, the choice is yours.

Ensuring a good night's sleep

It's the night before the interview. You've done all of your practical and psychological preparation and now all you need is a good night's sleep to feel sharp and confident on the big day. You may find yourself thinking, 'I really *have* to get a good night's sleep. Tomorrow is a big day and I need to be in top form.' Does this sound familiar? Have you ever told yourself that you *really* need to get to sleep because of important challenges the next day (a presentation, an exam, a vital meeting)? Understandable though this tendency is, it's usually counterproductive to *demand* that you get a good night's sleep, as you'll probably get the opposite result (similar to trying to block out any anxious thoughts or feelings, as we saw earlier). Picture the following scenario:

You turned out the light 10 minutes ago but your mind is still alert and you find yourself thinking, 'I've *got* to get to sleep or I'll screw up the interview tomorrow.' This thought triggers anxiety and leads to a shot of adrenaline coursing through your body. You start to notice your heart beating and you focus on other physical symptoms of anxiety (there's very little to distract you lying in bed in total darkness). This has been going on for a while and you're beginning to worry about how late it's getting so you glance at the alarm clock. '*Oh no.* It's one o'clock in the morning and I still haven't got to sleep.' More anxiety and another shot of adrenaline. By now you're getting desperate and you try to block out the thoughts about the interview and the day ahead but, as we know, blocking out thoughts leads to a re-bound effect and the thoughts just keep coming back. So now you're getting even more worried and telling yourself, 'This is *terrible*! How can I switch my mind off?' And so it goes on until you finally fall asleep only to be woken by the alarm very soon after.

Let's rewind the scenario and try things differently.

You've turned out the light and you haven't fallen asleep for a while – you're getting concerned about the implications for the interview next day. Instead of *demanding* that you get to sleep you'd be better off adopting *flexible preferences* (as I described in Chapter 1). You could tell yourself that even if you don't manage to sleep a wink all night, you'll still manage to do well at the interview because the adrenaline will make you alert just when you need it to – you could always have a strong cup of coffee as well. This may sound counterintuitive but if you stop engaging in *all-or-nothing thinking*, you may just take the psychological pressure off yourself to get to sleep and break the vicious cycle. By now you may be tempted to look at the alarm clock to check the time: Don't do it! Constant clock watching is a common feature of insomnia and many people get into the habit of monitoring the time throughout the night without even realising it. The problem with this is that you become fixated with how late it is and how little sleep you're going to get, leading to further anxiety. It is far better to place the clock at an angle where you can't see the time – the alarm will still wake you in the morning.

If you are feeling a little restless, it's not a good idea to start focussing excessively on any physical sensations of agitation like increased heartbeat or raised body temperature, as this will simply lead you into an inevitable vicious cycle of checking followed by worrying, leading to heightened arousal. Just acknowledge these sensations without judging them as *awful* and turn your attention to the diaphragmatic breathing technique I outlined earlier in this chapter, letting your thoughts drift away whilst gently bringing your attention back to your breath. You can also combine this approach with the techniques I described in the first visualisation exercise. This time instead of creating a virtual experience of the interview, use your imagination to create the most relaxing, calming experience you can think of – perhaps recalling a particular holiday. As with the imaginary interview, engage all five senses. Take yourself back to that beautiful beach looking at the sea glistening serenely as you hear the waves gently lapping nearby. You can feel the warmth of the sun beaming down on you and soothing your limbs and you can smell the pleasant fragrance of the sea breeze and suntan lotion. Your limbs feel pleasantly heavy and you feel drowsy and full of well-being. Taking yourself to an imaginary calm place combined with gentle diaphragmatic breathing will distract you from any anxious thoughts about the next day and activate you parasympathetic nervous system – you may find yourself drifting off to sleep before long. Let me share with you a number of other strategies you can put in place for getting a good night's sleep before the interview (and at any other time).

Unwind before bedtime

You may be tempted to carry on preparing for the interview right up to the last minute before bedtime. Even though further preparation may be unnecessary at this stage, it feels as though you're doing something and the activity offers a distraction from worrying about the interview. The problem with this approach is that your mind will be highly active when you go to bed and not sufficiently calm as a prelude to sleep. The problem will be further exacerbated if you use your computer or laptop. Research has shown that white light from computers and TVs disrupts our natural circadian rhythm by sending a message to our brains that it's still daytime and we should be awake. You need to wind down at least two hours before bedtime and avoid strenuous physical or mental activities to avoid excessive arousal. If you do watch TV, try to avoid content that's likely to increase arousal levels, like horror films or thrillers. Try to consume your last meal around four hours before you go to bed or your digestive system will still be working while you're trying to sleep. An optimum strategy for winding down would include a warm bath, listening to relaxing music, subdued lighting and possibly reading an undemanding book before bedtime. Above all, avoid leaving the task of preparing for the interview to the night before as you run the risk of getting yourself into an agitated state before bedtime.

Cut out alcohol and caffeine

Try to avoid all caffeinated drinks four to ideally six hours before bedtime, as they act as stimulants on the nervous system, making it harder to fall asleep or disrupting sleep patterns. (These include obvious sources of caffeine such as coffee, tea and energy drinks). Other seemingly innocuous beverages also contain caffeine, including chocolate cocoa (often considered a relaxing bedtime drink), iced tea and cola drinks. Also, many people don't realise that some painkillers and cold or flu remedies contain caffeine, so it's worth checking the packaging.

Alcohol can be a tempting option if you want to unwind and although it can make you feel relaxed before bedtime and usher in sleep, during the course of the night it will disturb your slumber. It will cause you to wake more frequently (not least due to needing the bathroom, as alcohol is a diuretic) and have a detrimental effect on the quality of your sleep so that you are less likely to awake feeling refreshed and mentally alert. The other trap you can fall into is that alcohol *disinhibits*. You may start with the best of intentions by resolving to restrict yourself to one or two drinks on the eve of an interview to 'soothe your nerves'. After consuming even this moderate an amount, you may convince yourself that another couple of drinks will make you relax even more – and why not stay up watching that interesting programme on TV? It'll take your mind off things. The unintended consequence of your unwinding strategy will be a hangover on the day of the interview or, at the very least, less energy and impaired cognitive functioning. A glass of wine with your evening meal is fine, as your body will have time to process the alcohol, but try to avoid anything else nearer bedtime.

If you can't sleep, get up and do something

If you find yourself lying in bed feeling totally alert and struggling to get to sleep after more than 20 minutes, it's advisable to get up, go into another warm room with subdued lighting and engage in a soothing activity like reading something undemanding or listening to relaxing music. Although this approach may sound counterintuitive, if you continue to lie in bed willing yourself to get to sleep and worrying about the consequences, you're more likely to trigger the vicious cycle we considered earlier in this section, resulting in increased anxiety and adrenaline. Reading something bland is particularly helpful as it will take your mind off the problem of getting to sleep without overstimulating your mind. You may also notice that your eyes become tired, gradually sending a signal to your brain that it's time to sleep. When you find yourself feeling drowsy, it's time to return to bed.

Optimise your sleep environment

One of the consequences of modern life is that the world of information technology increasingly encroaches upon the sanctuary of the bedroom. Many people watch TV in bed or use laptops and mobile phones. As I mentioned, the white light from TVs, laptops and even mobile phones will disrupt your circadian rhythm. It's also important to remove all reminders of work, clutter or anything else that's likely to trigger worry, exclude light and set an ambient temperature that's slightly cool. If you're unfortunate enough to live in a noisy environment or have inconsiderate neighbours, you may find that using foam or wax earplugs can offer you a temporary solution.

Ideally you need to create a relaxing environment in your bedroom that you associate with just two things: sleep and sex. Incidentally, the latter activity may be conducive to a good night's sleep before an interview as the act itself releases oxytocin and vasopressin – hormones that induce feelings of calm, well-being and bonding. It'll also take your mind off the interview.

On the day: act as if you are supremely confident

If you've tried all of the strategies that I've outlined and still find yourself feeling excessively nervous on the day of the interview, you could try *acting as if* you are supremely confident (but not arrogant, grandiose or unrealistic). This technique is sometimes described as 'fake it to make it'. You may feel sceptical about this approach, but consider the following. You now know that negative thinking styles can lead to an increase in anxiety and subsequent physiological consequences. This holds true of *behaviour*. If your body posture, actions and tone of voice reflect an anxious state, you are sending a strong signal to your brain that something is wrong, triggering more anxiety. The converse is true when you adopt a confident posture and use confident gestures and tone of voice *in spite* of feeling anxious. Suddenly your brain registers these positive behaviours and concludes that things must be going OK, leading to a virtuous cycle of increased confidence and reduced anxiety. But how do you go about finding the most helpful behaviours to adopt?

You could start by reviewing the helpful *behavioural consequences* we identified together as part of our ABC formulation of your forthcoming interview at the start of this chapter and use them in conjunction with the balanced, empowering thoughts also identified. How would you prefer to act in a confident way at the interview and what sort of behaviours could you engage in?

If you find it difficult to come up with ways in which you could think or act confidently at the interview, consider other people you admire and have observed to be outwardly confident. Think of how they would act, speak and think at the interview and try to *model* these behaviours. You can even assume the role of a celebrity you admire who embodies the qualities you wish to project at interview as part of this technique.

Robing plays a very important psychological role in helping people assume an identity. Many actors, including Laurence Olivier, claim that when they put on the costume of the character they are about to play, it is the starting point for feeling that they *are* the character. Interestingly, trainees with the Metropolitan Police Service in London are required to wear uniforms from the outset weeks before they are seen in public to help them gradually assimilate into their role by forming a new self-concept of themselves as police officers. If you've thought carefully about what to wear during the interview, you will have studied the dress code of the organisation you aspire to work for. When you put on your 'robes' for the interview, focus on assuming the role of the professional you want to be and the image you want to project, embodying qualities that the organisation you aspire to will desire.

In the next chapter, we'll examine the most important things you can do to achieve success in life: identifying your personal values and choosing a career that matches them.

If you forget everything else I've taught you in this chapter, remember this:

1   Nervousness at interviews is normal. Accept it and use it to your advantage – don't fight the elephant!
2   If you've revved yourself up with anxiety, put your foot on the break with calm breathing.
3   Manage an external focus of attention throughout the interview to keep you calm and alert.

4   What you imagine can trigger a helpful or unhelpful physiological response – the choice is yours.
5   Imagining a positive experience at interview will give you the resources to perform optimally.
6   Act as if you are extremely confident – the feeling will follow.

References

Cumming, J. and Ramsey, R. (2008). 'Sport imagery interventions'. In S. Mellalieu and S. Hanton (eds), *Advances in applied sports psychology: a review*, pp. 5–36. London: Routledge.

Darwin, C. (2011). *The origin of the species*. Collins Classics.

Dawkins, R. (2006). *The selfish gene*. Oxford University Press.

Goleman, D. (1996). *Emotional intelligence*. Bloomsbury Publishing.

Hackmann, A., Bennett-Levy, J. and Holmes, E. A. (2011). *Imagery in cognitive therapy*. Oxford University Press.

Haidt, J. (2006) *The happiness hypothesis: putting ancient wisdom to the test of modern science*. Arrow Books.

Siegel, D. (2013). *Mindsight*. Oneworld Publications.

Chapter 3

Making the right career decision

Gerard Egan (2002) has influenced the world of career counselling and professionals in the field throughout the world follow his recommendations when supporting clients in decision making. When faced with a major decision in your life, you need to engage in three vitally important processes.

Information gathering: If you are thinking about changing your career or embarking upon a career for the first time, you need to research your area of interest thoroughly so that you can make an *informed* decision. Although this sounds like obvious advice, many people set out on a course of academic study or training without researching what is required for entry into their intended occupation. They become enthusiastic with their newfound idea, feel as though they are going in the right direction and hope that the details will sort themselves out along the way. This is the equivalent to setting out on a journey without planning the route or calculating how much fuel you need. For example, many people embark on expensive, professionally marketed counselling courses in the hope that they will eventually be able to make a living as a counsellor. At a later stage they find that the course they have invested in is not recognised for the purposes of professional accreditation in their chosen field. Also, they find that there are a number of different types of counselling/therapy and other approaches would be better suited to their temperament and values. Enthusiasm about a new career direction needs to be tempered with information gathering and careful analysis.

If you live in the UK, a good place to start information gathering is at the government funded national career services website www .nationalcareersservice.direct.gov.uk (at the time of publication). Here you can find 800 different job profiles giving details of academic requirements, potential salaries and the level of competition for vacancies. The website hosts a variety of tools that can assist you with your research including a skills check and job hunting applications. You can even speak to an accredited career adviser over the telephone between the hours of 8:00 am to 10:00 pm seven days a week and all free of charge. Similar government funded agencies may be available free of charge in other countries, but do check that they offer *impartial* advice. Professional bodies are also a good source of information (e.g. the Institute of Chartered Accountants) and provide detailed advice on entry requirements and professional accreditation. Bear in mind that if you obtain support from a careers adviser of any description, they will usually have *general* knowledge of a wide range of occupations. You can use them as a resource but it's up to you to gain expertise in your chosen area of interest. It's far better to make the effort at this stage than waste time and money following the wrong path – and one that may bitterly disappoint you by leading to a dead end.

Analysis: Once you have gathered as much information as you can on your chosen occupation within the time available, you then need to process this data by considering the implications of different career or study options. Part of this process will require you to be brutally honest with yourself and *reality test* any assumptions you have made about your chosen career path. Have you checked the entry requirements in detail and are you reasonably confident that you can meet them? Can you afford the costs of retraining and do your life circumstances enable you to commit to this course of action wholeheartedly? Have you discussed your ambitions with significant others? I once had a client who was a very successful, but disillusioned, sales representative for a medical company. He left his job and enrolled in a course as a trainee plumber without telling his wife. You can probably guess the outcome. It's always worth developing *contingency plans* as part of your overall strategy. Let's say you want to study medicine but you're not 100 per cent certain you'll meet the course entry requirements. What other medical careers could you consider as a back-up plan with less challenging entry requirements? It's at this point that you need to be honest with yourself about your motivation for choosing a particular career direction. For example, many people consider medicine because of the status associated with the career rather than the desire to help others. There's nothing wrong with this desire and acknowledging it will help to develop suitable contingency plans. I'll talk about helping you to identify your personal values later on in this chapter.

Making a choice: If you've analysed the information in the way I've described, you will have hopefully reached the stage where you have a number of potential options available to you, requiring a final decision and commitment to act. Having advocated a *rational* approach thus far, I'd like you to pay attention to how you are feeling about your potential options *emotionally*. If you detect mixed feelings or some resistance, you may be experiencing the psychological condition known as *ambivalence*: the simultaneous existence of two opposed and conflicting attitudes or emotions. This is a very common reaction that people experience when faced with making major decisions in life and part of the reason for this uncomfortable feeling is that when you commit to a decision, you inevitably close down other options – often referred to by psychologists as the *Rubicon model* (Baumeister and Tierney, 2011). The Rubicon is a small river in northeastern Italy and in 49 BC it separated Rome from Gaul. The victorious general Julius Caesar returned with his army and knew that crossing the river would represent an act of insurrection against the Senate for which he could be executed (Marr, 2012). But he made the decision to cross the Rubicon with his army (hence the phrase), causing Consul Pompey to flee, and brought down the Roman republican constitution. Your decision may have less dire consequences at stake, but you need to clarify any feelings of ambivalence before you act, as these nagging doubts will act as a drain on your motivation – rather like driving a car with the handbrake on. A good way of flushing out any reservations you may hold about a potential decision is to construct a *cost and benefit analysis* (CBA). Let me give you an example of a cost and benefit analysis I worked on with a client.

Richard's choice

Richard is 42 and works as an operations manager in a 'not for profit' company that provides training courses for the long-term unemployed. He has become increasingly disillusioned with his job. When Richard started work with the company 10 years ago, he was very ambitious and wanted to work his way up to a senior management position. He achieved this goal and is well-paid, has a company car, but feels that his organisation is increasingly focussed on expansion and profit (in spite of being a 'not for profit' company) rather than the well-being of its clients. Also, he is increasingly required to work long hours writing reports in the evening and weekends at home. Richard was originally attracted to the company because it provided him with the opportunity to work directly with unemployed clients and help them to find employment or training. He has recently seen an advert with the National Health Service (NHS) for the role of trainee psychological therapist in his area. Richard has a psychology degree and has had some experience of counselling within a previous role. He is married with two young children and his wife works full time as a secondary school teacher. They have a joint mortgage on the family home. If Richard succeeds in gaining a trainee position with the NHS, he will have to take a significant reduction in salary and commute through a busy part of London.

By undertaking a detailed cost and benefit analysis (Table 3.1 below), Richard was able to mentally unpack a number of concerns he had about making his career decision and articulate some doubts that had been just below his level of awareness. Instead of endlessly chasing these concerns around in his head with no resolution, Richard was able to get an overview of the potential advantages and disadvantages for himself and his family in both the short term and long term, depending on which decision he made at this important stage in his career.

Richard realised that the short-term disadvantages associated with his potential career change were predominantly *material* costs and that the

Table 3.1 Richard's cost and benefit analysis

Costs and benefits of: retraining to be a trainee psychological therapist	
Costs (disadvantages)	Benefits (advantages)
Short-term *For self:* Significant reduction in salary Loss of company car Longer commute to work Risk of failing the training course	**Short-term** *For self:* Opportunity to participate in a high quality training course in a subject area that is intellectually stimulating New career direction that would be more consistent with personal values
For others: Less money for the family Having to leave home earlier and return later due to commute	*For others:* Spending less time writing reports at home and more time with the children
Long-term *For self:* Possible uncertainty around future government funding for mental health care	**Long-term** *For self:* Opportunities to develop a second career as a psychological therapist after training Possibility of setting up a private practise to supplement income
For others: Reduced income until promotion or qualified for private practise	Developing a second career consistent with personal values
	For others: Possibility of applying for NHS jobs in other parts of the country with cheaper housing and better education provision A happier, less stressed husband and father

salary and company car had kept him trapped in a job that he increasingly disliked. The greatest advantages in both the short and long term that resonated with him were choosing a career direction that was more consistent with his current personal values. The process also prompted an open discussion between Richard and his wife about how unhappy they had both become and about the increasingly negative impact of his job on family life. This led to further discussion on how the career change could lead to a number of possibilities for the family including moving to other parts of the country with cheaper housing and better educational provision for the children. Richard's wife had always been able to apply for teaching positions elsewhere but Richard's role had become specialised and limited in terms of career mobility. By retraining as a psychological therapist, he would have the opportunity to apply for similar NHS jobs in other parts of the country. This gave them both a positive vision for the future. The final obstacle that confronted them was the prospect of reduced income in the short and medium term. Richard and his wife calculated their joint income, taking into account his reduction in salary during the traineeship, and realised that by budgeting more carefully and taking less expensive holidays, they could manage until he qualified. The cost and benefit analysis had shown them that, overall, the risks and sacrifices were worth it for the positive changes they could make in their lives. You can carry out a similar cost and benefit analysis on any major life decision, including career direction. A blank version of the CBA worksheet can be found at Appendix 4.

Be SMART with your goals

Having 'crossed the Rubicon' and made a commitment to your decision, the next step is to take action. Gerard Egan (2002) observed that planning to take action should not be confused with taking action: without action, a plan for change just becomes a wish list. If you've come up with some goals, you now need to operationalise them into a range of tactics that will help you to stay motivated and focussed when the going gets tough. To stand the best chance of achieving your goals, you need to make them 'SMART':

S – pecific
M – easurable
A – ttainable
R – ealistic
T – ime bound

Specific

Your goals need to be clearly specified. Outlining vague ambitions like, 'getting a better paid job' or 'seeking a more senior position' will give you a sense of which direction to take but it won't help you to take action. You need to articulate *exactly* what you want to aim for. You can use Richard's goals as a guide:

- To apply for the position of trainee psychological therapist with the National Health Service (NHS) in central London
- To develop a budget for one year taking into account reduced income
- To develop a detailed plan on obtaining professional accreditation post-training

One of the main benefits in specifying detailed goals is that the process will enable you to outline the various steps needed to achieve your aims. You will also derive a motivational benefit by breaking down a potentially daunting task into a series of achievable steps. Once you start on the first task, you will generate the momentum to carry you onto the next.

Measurable

If you devise specific goals, you will be better able to measure ongoing achievement at each step along the way. Measuring progress will help you to stay focussed, and these minor victories will strengthen motivation to achieve your ultimate aim. Measuring Richard's first goal will be straightforward: he either obtains a traineeship with the NHS or he doesn't. His second goal, however, requires additional work if he and his family are to manage financially throughout the year:

- To monitor the family budget each month and obtain a positive balance between income and expenditure

Attainable

When you evaluate what is attainable in terms of your goals, you need to be brutally honest with yourself in assessing your *current* or *potential* skills and abilities. Richard had a degree in psychology and some counselling experience but recognised that he needed to obtain additional training on the way to making his career change. It's also very important for you to consider whether the goals you aspire to are congruent with your personal values, otherwise you run the risk of experiencing *ambivalence* and that will act as a drain on your motivation and levels of energy. If you're not aware of your personal values, I'll help you to define them later in this chapter.

Realistic

Ideally, you need to set goals that will take you slightly outside of your comfort zone, stretch your abilities and excite you. Setting overambitious goals runs the risk of failure and demotivation. However, if you set your sights too low, the prospect of achieving the goal will provide little motivation. Richard's goals were realistic because he had the foundation skills and knowledge to achieve them along with the support of his family. He acknowledged that achieving these goals would be challenging but the prospect of a new career provided sufficient motivation.

Time bound

It's essential to create a timeframe setting out when your goals need to be achieved by. If you fail to do this, your goals will remain mere aspirations with no sense of urgency driving you to take action. Many people make the mistake of waiting until they feel sufficiently motivated to take the first steps towards achieving their goal – this usually leads to procrastination, endlessly putting off the task. One of the most powerful CBT methods used with depressed clients (who *really* lack motivation) is an approach called *behavioural activation* (Martell, 2010) and its central principle is:

> *Act according to a plan, not a mood*

If you set timescales as part of your action plan, you can tell yourself to 'just do it!' as the deadline approaches. As a guide, aim to set short-term goals within the next few days or by the end of the following week. Medium-term goals can range from a week up to six months and long-term goals can be completed any time between six months to a year. The main thing to bear in mind when creating a timeframe is to give yourself enough time to achieve your goals without creating undue stress, but take out any slack in your plan so that you feel a constant sense of forward momentum and energy.

I've included an example of Richard's timeframe that you can adapt when mapping out your short, medium and long-term goals.

Richard's long-term goal:	**Time frame:**
To get a job as a qualified psychological therapist following training	1 year
Richard's short-term goals:	**Time frame:**
Register with the National Health Service vacancy website	Tomorrow
Read latest government policy on mental health strategy	Monday
Review CV and draft job application against job description and person specification	Wednesday
Complete job application online and submit	Friday
Richard's medium-term goals:	**Time frame:**
Develop a budget for one year taking into account reduced income	Within 2 weeks
Develop a detailed plan on obtaining professional accreditation post-training	Within 4 weeks
Research potential areas in the UK with cheaper housing and good secondary education provision	Within 8 months
Research potential NHS employers recruiting psychological therapists	Within 9 months

Maintaining your motivation

Once you have worked through any ambivalence and committed to a course of action with SMART goals, you need to ensure that you maintain your original level of enthusiasm. It's highly likely that you will encounter challenges and experience some boredom when completing the necessary tasks in your plan and it's at these moments that your enthusiasm is likely to dwindle and you risk losing momentum. It's helpful if you can anticipate potential obstacles to achieving your goal and develop contingency plans for dealing with these before you embark on your journey. The biggest challenge you may experience along the way is declining motivation to carry on when the going gets tough and even the temptation to give up striving towards your goal completely. Be proactive and pre-empt the likelihood of this occurring by following these principles.

Know why you're putting yourself through this: It will help you to remain focussed on the pursuit of your goal if you can continually remind yourself *why* you made this commitment in the first place. When your motivation falters, review your original cost and benefit analysis or the thinking process that led you to commit to this course of action. Often a vivid mental image of what your personal success looks, sounds and feels like will motivate you to carry on when you're at low ebb. I'll talk more about this in the next section. You can also make a *Ulysses pact* – a strong intention to bind yourself to a future course of action. Ulysses (Greek name, Odysseus), was king of Ithaka in ancient Greece and the hero of Homer's *Odyssey* (Rieu, 1991). He wanted to hear the songs of the sirens on his epic voyage home. The sirens were the original femme fatales – exotic creatures who lured sailors to their doom on the rocky coast of their island. Ulysses commanded his men to stop their ears with wax to prevent the sirens from beguiling them to sail their ship onto the rocks and told the crew to tie him to the mast so that he would be restrained from jumping overboard – hence, the term 'Ulysses pact'. He ordered his men to keep the ship to its course no matter what happened and to ignore any orders to the contrary. Ulysses was driven temporarily insane by the sirens' song but his men obeyed, the ship kept its course and he survived the deadly temptation. You could make a Ulysses pact with yourself from the outset of your 'voyage' not to be lured onto the rocks of apathy when you hear the siren call to give up on your goal and save yourself the discomfort that's an inevitable part of achieving most important objectives in life.

Keep your goals in sight and don't let them overwhelm you: It's helpful to continually review your goals and, if necessary, break them down into smaller bite-sized tasks when your motivation flags. For example, one of Richard's medium term goals was to develop a budget for one year taking into account reduced income. This could be separated further into different steps:

1   Create Excel spreadsheet for annual budget.
2   Review previous year's expenditure and enter appropriate budget headings (e.g. travel, food, mortgage).
3   Profile estimated monthly expenditure for the year.
4   Enter projected income for each month.

Record and reward: Breaking down goals into the smallest manageable steps will prevent you from feeling overwhelmed psychologically. It's also vitally important to celebrate every small step along the way.

When you reward yourself for achievement, your brain produces dopamine, a neurotransmitter that is associated with reward and motivation. Also, it makes you feel good, which is why so many people take recreational drugs to stimulate dopamine. In psychological terms you are engaging in *positive reinforcement*: rewarding these minor successes will train your brain to seek out further achievement for another dopamine hit. If you want an image to help you remember this strategy, look no further than *Pavlov's dogs*. Ivan Pavlov was a Russian physiologist and is world famous for his groundbreaking work in *classical conditioning* (Saunders, 2006). His early experiments involved giving a dog meat powder and ringing a bell several times. Eventually the dog began to associate the sound of the bell with the taste of the meat powder so that just ringing the bell would cause the dog to salivate. Recording and rewarding 'mini-goals' will establish the same positive association in your brain and strengthen your motivation.

But I don't know which path to take!

If you have some idea of the direction you wish to take in terms of your career development, the process is reasonably straightforward. Whether you are just starting out after completing formal education or seeking a complete career change after several years, if you've settled on an occupational area, the necessary steps can be summarised as follows:

- Researching your chosen career
- Matching job availability against your skills, qualifications and temperament
- Contingency planning (in case you don't gain entry into your preferred occupation)
- Applying for opportunities
- Reviewing outcomes and refining your strategy (if you don't succeed initially)

A far more challenging situation arises when you have no idea which direction to take and you're hoping that, eventually, the answer will reveal itself to you in a moment of inspiration. It's at this point that you might feel envious of the lucky minority of people who have a *calling* – an innate sense of being drawn towards a particular career. Many people try to resolve this common dilemma by visiting career advisers and using psychometric tests and occupational interest guides. These approaches are worth trying as they may generate inspiration or at least additional ideas for further reflection. They fall under the category of *rational* decision making – left brain activity engaged in sifting information and making logical interpretations. It's also worth engaging your more emotionally connected right brain if you seek inspiration and two creative approaches that can help you to do this are *visualisation techniques* and *identifying your personal values*. I will now explore these methods with you in detail.

Building a powerful vision for the future

We explored the use of visualisation technique in Chapter 2 when preparing for interviews or other challenging events. The aim of this approach was to undertake a 'virtual rehearsal' of future-based events to make them seem more familiar and, by doing so, reduce anxiety about the outcome. The purpose of the current exercise is to stimulate your imagination. Sometimes it's important for us to dream of how our future lives could be in order to obtain a sense of direction. If we can create a powerful vision that moves us to take action, the practical tasks and information needed to realise this vision will often follow. Building a vivid image of yourself engaged in a rewarding career and enjoying an associated lifestyle will give you the motivation to take the necessary steps to realising your vision.

You may recall times in your childhood when you fantasised about the type of job you would engage in as an adult later in life. Many of these fantasies are naïve and change over time, but some individuals are fortunate enough to experience the sense of calling I described earlier and realise their childhood ambitions, often after overcoming a number of hurdles including discouragement from parents and significant others. Unfortunately, most of us lose the childlike ability to create imagined future scenarios as we grow up because we are encouraged to think 'rationally and realistically' by authority figures including parents, teachers and older family members. As children, we often accept what adults tell us without question – they're older than us so they must know better. The problem is that this advice may lead to low aspirations due to social or cultural circumstance that the child is born into. Even if that isn't the case, the encouragement by adults to 'think sensibly' about the future increases our tendency to self-censor and restricts creative thought about what we could become. In spite of these restrictions, we still indulge in daydreams but dismiss these as whimsical fantasies without realising the potency of this activity.

I'd like to remind you of what we explored in Chapter 2 when I introduced you to the first visualisation exercise when preparing for interview. Our ancient ancestors developed the ability to visualise past and future events and this enabled them to survive and flourish. Our unique ability to construct reality from the power of our imagination is the source of all human creativity, but we often underestimate the power of this process and don't fully appreciate the gift we have been given. The following exercise is intended to revive and strengthen this ability and provide you with a means of developing a compelling vision for your future career.

Step 1

Find somewhere quiet where you are unlikely to be disturbed and sit comfortably. This exercise is most effective if practised with your eyes closed to help you focus and concentrate. It will be helpful for you to revisit the relaxation exercise outlined in Chapter 2 to enter into a calm state of mind and body by concentrating on your breath. It will also help you to gain distance from the many competing demands on your attention so that you can focus your mind on creative processes. As with many of the exercises described in this book, don't try too hard – let your thoughts disperse and gently bring your attention back to your breathing. If thoughts come back to you, just notice them and let them drift away. Some people find it helpful to imagine their thoughts as clouds passing by.

Step 2

Once your mind is calm and you are in a relaxed state, gradually let your mind wander and begin to fantasise how you would like your life to be if there were no limitations. If you find yourself interrupting this flow by considering practical issues, let these thoughts go for the time being and concentrate on enjoying your fantasy of a life lived completely on your terms. After you have become immersed in this fantasy for a while, begin to notice the type of work you are doing and the kind of home you are living in. What else do you notice about the clothes you are wearing, the people around you and the various locations you find yourself in? Take yourself through your ideal day at work from leaving your home to returning or engaging in social activities.

Step 3

Start to notice subtle details as your fantasy develops:

- Look around at your work colleagues and the location–what can you see and hear?
- What does your home look like? Are you alone or do you share it with someone?
- How does your day unfold: do you get up early or late?
- What can you smell, touch and taste as part of your fantasy?
- Tune into your emotions–are you feeling calm, excited, content?

Step 4

Enjoy being in this place for as long as feels natural to you and eventually bring your attention back to the present. Notice the feeling of the chair you are sitting in, remind yourself of where you are and gradually open your eyes. Take your time to orient yourself back into the present and gently move your limbs. Stay in a calm state of mind, don't rush off just yet. Sit and reflect on your experience and consider any insights you may have gained. What does your vision for the future say about your personality and your unmet needs? Can you think of any careers that would help you to realise some or most of the elements of your fantasy? What next steps could you take to research these careers?

If you found this to be a positive experience, you may wish to practise the exercise several times in the way that I've described. You can continually nurture your vision of the future at any spare moment in the day, for instance, travelling on public transport, shopping or standing in a queue. Holding a vivid image of your ideal future will act as an unconscious compass in your mind, providing you with a sense of direction and enabling you to draw on the internal resources needed to make it a reality. Once you figure out the practical steps needed to embark on your journey, the purpose of your vision changes from being inspirational to motivational. Although the details of your personal vision may change many times, it will light the way forward and remind you of the reason you embarked on your journey in the first place. The next section will help you to make your vision for the future even more compelling by helping you to identify your core values.

Personal values and career satisfaction

Most Japanese martial arts have the word 'do' appended to them. Examples that you may have come across include judo, karate-*do*, aiki*do*, ken*do* and if you have ever practised a Japanese martial art you will inevitably have trained in a *dojo* – translated literally as a 'way place' (Williams, 1975). This notion of following a way, or path, through life underlies most Japanese martial arts. It stresses the importance of setting out on a journey that concludes only when life ends and attaining knowledge and wisdom along the way; you could describe this in terms of seeking enlightenment through experiences good and bad. I want to invite you to regard your career in the same way. In fact, many dictionaries define the word 'career' in terms of a path or progress through life. But before you take the first or next step on your journey, it will be helpful for you to define your personal values.

You may never have considered in any depth what your personal values are, or it may have been some time since you reflected on them. You may have a vague sense of what's important in your life but struggle to articulate these values succinctly. Yet obtaining a keen sense of your personal values is vitally important for a number of reasons. Stephen Covey, author of *The Seven Habits of Highly Effective People* (Covey, 1999), describes this process in terms of defining principles of personal leadership. His second key habit is *begin with the end in mind*, essentially, have a vision of what you want your life to be and follow this vision based on your personal values. At the start of the chapter devoted to this second habit, Covey invites you to imagine attending your own funeral and to consider what you would like friends and family members to say about you and your achievements in life. This exercise may prompt you to consider your personal values by holding the end of your life in mind and reflecting on what is truly important to you.

Another way of thinking about values involves developing a sense of mission in life. Most organisations develop a mission statement to encapsulate the shared values of the company and to define its direction of travel. If they adhere to these original principles, the organisation's strategies will flow from its principle values. When Anita Roddick founded The Body Shop, her organisation opened with the mission statement, 'To dedicate our business to the pursuit of social and environmental change', and her company's strategies reflect these values by ensuring that The Body Shop's stores and products promote human rights and

environmental issues. In the same way that companies use mission statements to give a collective sense of strategic direction, carefully defining
your personal values will make it easier to find the path, or career, you
want to take in life. If you find an occupation that gives you the opportunity to express these values, you have a much greater likelihood of
obtaining job satisfaction and, ultimately, a life well-lived.

Some fortunate individuals are naturally drawn to certain occupations early in life and, often without knowing it, their chosen careers
are an expression of their personal values. As I mentioned previously,
these people can be described as having a calling or vocation. You
can probably think of examples of people entering careers in medicine, teaching, politics and religious faiths. Very often, individuals who
are drawn to these careers possess strong values with regards to helping others and making a difference to society and they experience a
sense of fulfilment in their work because it is an outward expression
of their values. But the opposite is true of many unfortunate people
who labour away in jobs that make them deeply unhappy because their
role is incompatible with their personal values. If we go back to the
example of Richard, whom we met in Chapter 2, you may recall that
he was initially attracted to working for an organisation that gave him
the opportunity to help unemployed people find work. As the company
grew, its sense of mission changed from working for the benefit of the
client, first and foremost, to expansion and profit. Gradually Richard
became aware of a growing sense of unease and instead of looking
forward to work, he began to dread going in on a Monday morning.
Richard experienced with increasing frequency what he described as
an 'inner conflict' between what he was required to do on behalf of the
organisation (like making people redundant to increase profit margins)
and what he thought was 'the right thing to do'. Eventually Richard
took stock of his personal values and realised that continuing to work in
the organisation would make him increasingly unhappy in spite of the
material rewards. He realised that he needed a job that would help him
to express his personal values.

You can see from Richard's example why working in a job that conflicts
with your personal values can lead to what is described in psychology as
cognitive dissonance: a feeling of mental stress due to internal discord
between deeply held values or beliefs. But why does engaging in work
or other activities consistent with our personal values give us such a profound feeling of gratification and happiness? One possible explanation
is that when we engage in these activities, we experience a state of being

described as *flow*. I will now introduce you to this concept and describe its significance for your career and life in general.

Flow and job satisfaction

The psychologist Mihaly Csikszentmihalyi (pronounced 'cheeks sent me high') made a significant contribution to the field of psychology when he defined the concept of 'flow', a state of complete absorption in the moment when performing certain activities and the experience of a deep sense of gratification and mastery (Csikszentmihalyi, 2002). He lived quite an interesting life and his early experiences led to the discovery of this groundbreaking concept. Csikszentmihalyi is descended from Hungarian aristocracy and his father was the ambassador from Budapest residing in Rome. But after the Second World War the family lost its wealth when Hungary came under communist rule and Csikszentmihalyi's father had to leave the embassy and set up a restaurant to make a living. Young Mihaly developed an early interest in psychology by observing how some of his countrymen were plunged into depression and inertia after losing their former status while others thrived by rising above their challenging circumstances and helping others around them, much like Viktor Frankl's experiences in Auschwitz (Frankl, 1984). This early interest drove Csikszentmihalyi to search for meaning concerning the human condition in works of philosophy and religion and eventually the study of psychology in America, where he obtained a PhD and defined the concept of 'flow'.

You may have come across descriptions of flow in sports psychology where athletes describe it as being in 'the zone', completely absorbed in the moment whilst engaged in their specific skill. Not all activities leading to a flow experience have to be intensely physical. This state of absorption can also be obtained by practising sedentary activities such as playing chess or reading an intellectually stimulating book. Csikszentmihalyi has researched numerous examples of flow experiences, from car assembly workers to brain surgeons, and has noted that we are more likely to experience flow when the following conditions are present:

- The task we engage in is challenging and requires us to perform a skill
- We need to focus as much as possible on the activity we are engaged in
- We have clearly defined goals
- We get immediate feedback while we are engaged in the activity

Not all of these conditions have to be present for you to experience flow, but Csikszentmihalyi found that their prevalence leads to a heightened sense of being alive that results in:

- Deep, effortless absorption in the task
- A feeling of being in control
- Awareness of your 'self' fading away as you focus on the activity
- A feeling as though time is standing still

I'd like you to pause and think back over the most positive and memorable experiences you have had in your life. Try to think of a time when you were completely absorbed in the moment and consider whether what you experienced could be described as 'flow'. If you can bring to mind an example of this, think of how your life could be enriched by deliberately creating the conditions that would enable you to experience this profound sense of being fully alive in the present moment.

But why is this experience of flow so important for our mental well-being? Csikszentmihalyi made some very important observations about the human mind. He suggested that, without some form of training, most people find it difficult to focus their thoughts for more than a few minutes and, worse than that, our default state in terms of consciousness is what he describes as entropy, or internal disorder.

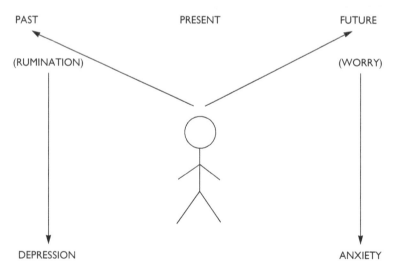

Figure 3.1 The mind's shifting focus of attention.

Consider your own state of mind for a moment. How much of your attention is usually focussed on the present and how much of it drifts back to past events or imagines future scenarios? Csikszentmihalyi realised that one of the unfortunate burdens of human consciousness is that our minds vacillate between the past and the future and we are seldom focussed on the present moment (Figure 3.1). Also, we tend to engage in two very unhelpful activities: *worry*, when our thoughts focus on potential negative future events, and *rumination*, when we brood on negative past events. Evolutionary psychologists have hypothesised that we have inherited these behaviours from our ancient ancestors because they were helpful in terms of our survival. Worrying about or imagining future hazards may have enabled hunter gatherers to anticipate dangers that lie ahead and formulate strategies for dealing with them. Ruminating about negative past experiences may have facilitated learning and the avoidance of making similar, possibly dangerous, mistakes. According to this theory we are 'hard-wired' to worry about the future and ruminate about the past but, unfortunately, these behaviours are seldom helpful for us in our twenty-first-century lives.

Worry about various future possibilities, often proceeded by 'what if?' statements, triggers anxiety and all its negative physiological consequences that we encountered in Chapter 2. This type of worrying is extremely common and unhelpful (Wells, 2008) because it focuses on *hypothetical* possibilities that may or may not happen ('What if I get made redundant at some time in the future?') and is very different from adopting a problem solving approach to real worries ('I've just received notice that I'm being made redundant next month and I need to find another job'). Rumination (derived from the Latin *ruminat*, literally to 'chew over') is a tendency to go over something in one's mind again and again and often leads to low mood or, in serious instances, depression (Martell, 2010). It is a very similar process to worry and is often characterised by 'if only...' statements. Rumination, sometimes referred to as brooding, gives the illusion of trying to gain insight into why something bad may have happened (e.g. the end of a significant relationship) but, like hypothetical worry, it seldom leads to practical problem solving or insight and keeps the individual locked into a cycle of gloomy thoughts.

One of the tragedies of the human condition is that many people go through their whole lives *partially* experiencing events because their mind is elsewhere. How many of us, towards the end of a holiday, have let our minds fast forward to our daily work routine and the many associated concerns we'll be returning to? We could be standing in one of the most beautiful places on earth but only be physically present because our mind is back in the workplace surveying the many tasks that have accumulated in our absence. Buddhist teaching refers to the capricious, disorganised state of our consciousness as 'monkey mind' (Dalai Lama, 1998) and advocates the practice of meditation to bring calm and order. Becoming completely absorbed in a meaningful activity and experiencing flow can give you respite from the constant mental chatter that we experience every day of our lives and will help you to get the most out of the present moment. But as well as being generally beneficial for our mental well-being, how does flow feature in the workplace?

Csikszentmihalyi conducted a fascinating experiment that measured subjects' experience of flow whilst at work and during leisure time using a technique called *experience sampling method* (ESM) (Csikszentmihalyi and LeFevre 1987, 1989). Subjects in the study were allocated pagers and prompted to record what they were doing at random times during the day and evening, including any thoughts or feelings they experienced and their level of absorption in the activity. This was a significant experiment as it involved thousands of participants from a range of socioeconomic and cultural backgrounds. The results of the experiment were startling: Data collected from the experience sampling method demonstrated that *the majority of participants in the study experienced far greater levels of flow at work than when engaged in leisure time activities.* This finding was counterintuitive as most people, when asked what they would rather be doing, expressed a preference for some type of leisure activity over work.

Professor Martin E. P. Seligman is one of the world's leading experts on positive psychology and a colleague of Csikszentmihalyi. He noted the findings of the experiment and theorised that the result may be due to the fact that watching television is one of the most popular leisure activities in America and that the average reported mood state whilst watching TV is *mild depression* (Seligman, 2002). This hypothesis could also be extended to Britain and Western Europe. Seligman builds on this interpretation of Csikszentmihalyi's experiment by suggesting that sustained and excessive indulgence in easily achieved hedonistic pleasures can be detrimental to psychological well-being in the long term, whilst engaging in the type of activities leading to the experience of flow will lead to psychological growth and well-being.

This makes sense in the context of addictions including drugs, alcohol, nicotine, gambling, binge eating and excessive shopping. Indulging in any addictive behaviour results in the brain releasing *dopamine*, a powerful neurotransmitter that plays a major part in human (and animal) motivation and reward drives (Siegel, 2013). Every time an addict snorts a line of cocaine, they receive a huge hit of dopamine leading to an intense feeling of euphoria. The big problem for addicts is that this huge and immediate *reward* for very little effort reinforces the unhelpful behaviour and depletes willpower, leading to a vicious cycle of addiction. Rising levels of obesity and alcohol consumption in many European countries (OECD, 2012) indicate that an increasing number of people are taking shortcuts to experience transient moments of happiness through consumption. I don't wish to make a value judgment about indulging in hedonistic pursuits, and Seligman also celebrates the value in experiencing pleasure too. It's more a question of striking a balance between indulging in pleasure and achieving personal growth: a constant tension within us that is part of the human condition.

Seligman illustrates how we can help ourselves by building what he calls 'psychological capital', an analogy he makes with economics. According to Seligman, when we indulge in hedonistic pleasures (a glass of wine, a piece of cake, a foot massage), we make a *withdrawal* in psychological terms. Although these are delightful experiences, indulged in excessively, they gradually deplete our willpower and resilience. These experiences are not an *investment* in that they do not lead to an accumulation of knowledge or personal growth. On the other hand, engaging in activities that lead to the experience of flow, Seligman hypothesises, leads to an increase in psychological resources (wisdom, resilience) that can be drawn on at some stage in the future. These helpful principles can be rendered into the following simple formula:

Indulgence in hedonistic pleasure = **withdrawal** of psychological capital

Participation in flow activities = **investment** of psychological capital

Seligman illustrates this concept by telling a story about one of his teachers who was given an exotic Amazonian lizard. He struggled to find food that his newly acquired pet would accept, and it began to starve to death in front of him. According to the story, the teacher came home one day and made one last desperate attempt to feed the lizard a ham sandwich he had bought for lunch, once again, without success. Feeling despondent, the teacher absentmindedly threw his newspaper on top of the sandwich and was startled when the lizard roused itself, ripped the paper to shreds and voraciously devoured the sandwich. The point Seligman makes is that the lizard needed to exercise its innate hunting and stalking abilities, acquired over thousands of years of natural selection, before it could devour its meal.

In one of his short stories, *The Hunger Artist* (Kafka, 1981), the German author Franz Kafka tells the tale of a circus performer whose art is to sit in a cage for weeks without eating. Eventually the audience tires of this spectacle and drifts away and the artist is gradually forgotten. Weeks pass and eventually someone visits the hunger artist who is at the point of fading away. He confesses to the person that his art has been a lie: It required no effort as he had never found the sustenance he sought. Seligman suggests that we as human beings have a profound need to exercise our more complex range of skills and virtues (that lead to the experience of flow) and that if we continually take shortcuts to easy, unearned gratification, we risk starving to death spiritually even though we are surrounded by increasing material wealth in the western world. Work offers us the opportunity to practice our innately human skills and achieve our greatest moments of satisfaction in life.

The idea that toil can ennoble us isn't completely original and goes all the way back to Max Webber's Protestant work ethic (Webber, 2012) or even further, to Aristotle's notion of the 'the good life' (Irvine, 2009). This view may seem somewhat anachronistic when regarded from a twenty-first-century individualistic perspective and, when going back to Csikszentmihalyi's experiment, the fact that the majority of people want to escape what they consider to be the tyranny of enforced employment. But the modern-day philosopher Alain de Botton (2009) reflects on our profoundly human need to engage in purposeful activity in *The Pleasures and Sorrows of Work* along with Harvard lecturer Tal Ben-Shahar. In his positive psychology book *Happier* (2008) Ben-Shahar maintains that even if the requirement to work for a living were taken away from us, we would still need to work in order to experience happiness in life. This is similar to the essence of Victor Frankl's logotherapy philosophy (Frankl, 1984), that we need a raison d'etre, a sense of purpose in life. The converse is true also. Recent research commissioned by the UK Department for Work and Pensions (Waddell and Burton, 2006; DWP, 2009) suggests that being unemployed can lead to deterioration in mental and physical health and there is a strong correlation between unemployment and increased mortality (Yuen and Balarajan, 1989). There are a number of reasons for this, not least because, deprived of the daily structure that work provides, the unemployed have huge amounts of time to worry and ruminate. There's also the individual's loss of self-concept – their sense of who they are as a person (Buss et al., 1983). Most people define themselves by their occupation ('I'm a mechanic', 'an accountant', 'a nurse') and when they lose this through ill health, redundancy or even retirement, they often experience a period of grieving for their former self.

Work provides traction (Haworth and Evans, 1987), the structure and routine that wards off what Csikszentmihalyi referred to as our descent into entropy when we don't have a sense of purpose. It also enables us, as Seligman has shown, to express our human values and experience flow. And our best chance of achieving this state and of experiencing profound satisfaction is to pursue work that is consistent with our personal values.

Identifying your personal values

If you can accurately identify your personal values and find an occupation that enables you to give them expression on a daily basis, your life will be enriched and purposeful. The *value focus inventory* in this chapter will enable you to explore different aspects of potential occupations to determine how closely they correspond with your personal values. What I mean by 'values' in this context is the principles and standards that you consider to be important in your life. They are different to goals and commitments, although some people confuse these with values. It might help you to think of your values collectively as a *compass* that will guide your actions and choices because you are consciously choosing to live according to your personal set of principles. It's also very important for you to be honest with yourself when identifying your personal values – they need to reflect what you consider to be of the utmost importance in your life. If making money and attaining power are important to you, then these are perfectly acceptable values in the same way that wanting to help others and support environmental issues are valid principles to live by. Identifying values should not be influenced by a desire to list principles that others might admire – they need to be personally authentic.

It's also possible that your priorities in life may have shifted during the passing of time. Key life events such as parenthood, beginning or ending significant relationships, experiencing illness or bereavement may all lead to a reordering of your priorities. In spite of this you may find it reassuring that your core values stay the same irrespective of life changes and it can be helpful to hold them in your mind during challenging periods. In the same way, your values may conflict with urgent priorities that arise and require compromise. For example, if one of your values is family life and you have urgent monetary needs, you may need to prioritise work until you are in a financially stable position before returning to a more balanced lifestyle.

The *value focus inventory* below (Table 3.2) will help you to examine specific aspects of work that could enable you to live according to your personal values. You will see that I have included a number of other life domains in which to consider your personal values. The 'Valued Focus' column provides examples of statements that can be adapted to express your values. A blank version of the inventory can be found at Appendix 5.

Table 3.2 Valued focus inventory

Area WORK Examples of work values	Valued focus
RANGE: Having a variety things to do	*Variation of activities is important to you—you find routine boring*
LOCATION: Where you work is important to you	*You may want to work close to where you live to reduce time spent travelling; or you may want to feel more connected with the local community*
SERENITY: You prefer to have few pressures or demands placed on you at work	*Feeling calm is very important—you find the experience of stress aversive*
COMPETITION: You enjoy competing against other individuals or organisations	*You thrive in a competitive environment and it provides you with a strong motivation to succeed*
AUTONOMY: You prefer minimal or no supervision	*You want to be your own boss and take responsibility for your decisions*
FLEXIBILITY: You prefer to plan work at your own convenience	*You want to be able to arrange your life around personal priorities other than work*
SOCIAL CONTACT: You like jobs that involve socialising with colleagues outside working hours	*You derive energy from being with like-minded people at work and enjoy socialising with them after hours*
DYNAMIC ENVIRONMENT: You enjoy high energy work	*You like a fast-paced, exciting work environment*
HIGH STATUS: Obtaining respect from others for the work you do is important to you	*Your job defines who you are as a person and you enjoy the prestige of having senior status*
INFLUENCE: You want your work to have a major impact on the lives of others	*You have strong convictions and find it gratifying to make key decisions*
INNOVATION: You want the opportunity to express your creativity at work	*You want to be able to express your sense of creativity through work*
RISK TAKING: You enjoy taking calculated risks as part of the role	*You are excited by taking risks, particularly if their success leads to rewards*
STIMULATION: You need work that gets you firing on all cylinders	*You find routine boring and need an environment that is highly energetic*
REMUNERATION: High monetary reward for your efforts—a bonus culture—is important to you	*You are highly motivated by material rewards and measure your success in this way*

Area	Valued focus
WORK	
Examples of work values	

CARING & COMPASSION: You have a sense of vocation for helping people individually or in groups	*The most rewarding aspect of the job is helping to improve the lives of others, possibly those more disadvantaged than yourself*
CAREER PROGRESSION OPPORTUNITY: You desire excellent prospects for advancement within your job	*You prefer to plan your career in terms of climbing the ladder to success, with clear routes for progression*
STRETCH: You flourish when challenged and under pressure	*You work best when your talents are stretched and you have to work to tight deadlines*
PREDICTABILITY: You enjoy a stable work environment with routines	*You prefer a secure career in which you are confident about your role and the structures within which you work*
TEAMWORK: You enjoy the creative energy of achieving objectives with others	*You enjoy collaborating with others and believe that you are able to achieve more working together*
PHYSICAL WORK: You want to be constantly on the move, sometimes requiring strength and stamina	*You prefer to be physically active as part of your work and feel energised by it*
SOLITARY LABOUR: You prefer isolation	*You prefer working alone as you find the company of others draining*
AESTHETIC: You work creatively and artistically	*You are artistic and need work that enables you to be creative in different domains*
COMMUNICATION: You excel at expressing concepts through the medium of language	*You feel in your element when you are able to communicate with others through the written or spoken word*
VALIDATION: Recognition for effort	*Having your efforts recognized by others is one of the most important reasons for working*
JOB SECURITY: You desire predictability about the future of your role	*You are risk averse and need the stability of predictable future employment*
EXTRAVERT: You derive energy from contact with others	*You feel at your best in the company of others and have excellent interpersonal skills*
EXACTITUDE: You enjoy working with precision	*You enjoy close attention to detail and take pride in producing highly accurate work*

(continued)

Table 3.2 Valued focus inventory (*continued*)

Area WORK Examples of work values	Valued focus
SOCIALLY CONSCIOUS: You want to work for the common good	*You need to make a contribution to society and the lives of others through your work*
MANAGERIAL: You want to take the lead	*You have a talent for leadership and organisation*
INFLUENCING: You have excellent negotiation skills	*You enjoy using influence and the power of persuasion with others*
KNOWLEDGE: You want to participate in lifelong learning	*You need a work environment that offers intellectual stimulation and opportunities for extending your skills and knowledge*
EXPERTISE: You desire the status conferred by mastering a specialty	*You are motivated by gaining mastery in a specific area of expertise and enjoy the status associated with your role.*

PERSONAL DEVELOPMENT
Consider how important the role of education and training are in your life by asking yourself:

- What new skills and qualifications do you wish to acquire?
- How much time are you prepared to commit?
- Will you train or study full-time, part-time or on-the-job?
- How much money are you prepared to contribute toward your personal development?

You value lifelong learning and are committed to devoting a significant amount of time on personal development

You regard paying for your personal development as a positive investment in your career

INTIMATE AND FAMILY RELATIONSHIPS
Reflect on what you want from current or future relationships:

- How much freedom do you want within your relationship?
- Do you prefer to spend most of your time with your partner engaging in shared activities?
- Is your preference for someone similar to yourself or do you believe that opposites attract?
- What are your guiding principles as a parent?
- What is of key importance in your relationships with your parents, siblings and other family members?

You want an intimate relationship that allows both you and your partner to have your mutual needs met, including developing your career

You draw strength from your family and balance work commitments to spend time with them

Area	Valued focus
WORK	
Examples of work values	

FRIENDSHIPS

When considering current or future friendships:

- Do you feel most at ease with a small number of friends that you have known for a long time and can 'be yourself' with?
- Do you welcome many friendships with a diverse range of people from different social backgrounds, occupations and who hold different views than you?
- What are the key things that you expect from your friends?
- What are your guiding principles in being a friend to others?

You prefer the company of a select number of friends that you have known for some time, with whom you feel comfortable and can confide in
Or
You have a wide network of friends with different personalities and interests and find varied company stimulating

FREE TIME AND LEISURE

Consider your main preferences with regards to how you spend your free time:

- Do you prefer to seek comfort and pleasure during your free time to recover from the rigours of work and life in general?
- Do you prefer being surrounded by nature or an urban environment?
- Do you derive energy from sports and other physically active pursuits in your free time?
- Do you obtain pleasure and relaxation from engaging in intellectual pastimes such as reading, theatre or studying?

You value free time and spend it wisely on a range of activities that give you pleasure, challenge and energise you and give you a sense of personal development

SPIRITUALITY

Reflect on whether you have what you consider to be spiritual values. These could include:

- Belief and practice in a religious faith
- Holding humanistic values
- Practising personally meaningful activities that feel transformative, such as meditation

You have spiritual convictions that guide your actions and engaging in spiritual activities gives you a sense of peace and connectedness to something greater than yourself

(continued)

Table 3.2 Valued focus inventory (*continued*)

Area WORK *Examples of work values*	*Valued focus*
PHYSICAL & MENTAL WELL-BEING Consider what's important to you in maintaining optimum physical and mental health: • Keeping physically fit and increasing stamina • Reducing stress through relaxing activities • Paying attention to diet and nutrition	*You invest time in your physical and mental well-being and find a balance between exercise and relaxation*

If you forget everything else I've taught you in this chapter, remember this:

1 You may feel *ambivalent* about a career decision – unpack your concerns using a cost and benefit analysis.
2 You stand the best chance of being happy at work if you choose a career that is congruent with your personal values.
3 Nurture an ideal vision of the future as your guiding light along the path you take in life.
4 Act according to a plan, not a mood, to maintain motivation.
5 Our minds have a tendency to switch between the future and the past – we find it difficult to stay in the present moment.
6 Experiencing 'flow' (being completely absorbed in the moment) can be one of the most satisfying experiences you have in life. Finding a job that is congruent with your values provides you with the best chance of experiencing 'flow' in the workplace.

References

Baumeister, R. F. and Tierney, J. (2011). *'Willpower': rediscovering our greatest strength*. Allen Lane.
Ben-Shahar, T. (2008). *Happier – can you learn to be happy?* McGraw-Hill Books.
Buss, T. F., Stevens Redburn, F., Waldron, J. (1983). *Mass unemployment: plant closing and community mental health*. SAGE.
Covey, S. (1999). *The 7 habits of highly effective people*. Simon Schuster.
Csikszentmihalyi, M. (2002). *Flow: the psychology of optimal experience*. Harper Perennial.

Csikszentmihalyi, M. and LeFevre, J. (1987). *The experience of work and leisure*. Paper presented at the Third Canadian Leisure Research Conference, Halifax, Nova Scotia, May 22–25.

Csikszentmihalyi, M., and LeFevre, J. (1989). *Optimal experience in work and leisure*. Journal of Personality and Social Psychology 56(5):815–22.

De Botton, A. (2009). *The pleasures and sorrows of work*. Penguin.

Egan, G. (2002). *The skilled helper*. Brooks/Cole.

Frankl, V. (1984). *Man's search for meaning*. Washington Square Press.

Haworth, J. T. and Evans, S. T. (1987). Meaningful activity and unemployment, in *Unemployed people – social and psychological perspectives* edited by David Fryer and Phillip Ullah. Open University Press.

Kafka, F. (1981). *Samtliche erzahlungen*. Fischer Tachenbuch Verlag.

Marr, A. (2012). *A history of the world*. Macmillan.

Martell, C. R., Dimidjian, S., and Herman-Dunn, R. (2010). *Behavioral activation for depression*. The Guilford Press.

OECD. (2012). Health at a glance: Europe 2012. OECD Publishing.

Rieu, E. V. (1991). *Homer: the Odyssey*. Penguin Classics.

Saunders, B. R. (2006). *Ivan Pavlov: exploring the mysteries of behaviour*. Enslow Publishers.

Seligman, M. E. P. (2002). *Authentic happiness*. Free Press.

Siegel, D. (2013). *Mindsight*. Oneworld Publications.

Waddell, G. and Burton, A. K. (2006). Is work good for your health and wellbeing? Commissioned by the Department for Work and Pensions.

Webber, M. (2012). *The Protestant ethic and the spirit of capitalism*. Renaissance Classics.

Wells, A. (2008). *Cognitive therapy of anxiety disorders*. Wiley.

Williams, B. (1975). *Know karate-do*. William Luscombe Publisher.

Yuen, P., and Balarajan, R. (1989). Unemployment and patterns of consultation with the general practitioner. *British Medical Journal* 298(6682): 1212–14.

Chapter 4

Using cognitive and behavioural approaches to succeed in the workplace

Stress-busting at work

According to the UK Health and Safety Executive (HSE, 2014), the total number of working days lost due to work-related stress, depression or anxiety was 11.3 million in 2013–2014, an average of 23 days per case of stress, depression or anxiety. The main activities that the HSE survey found as causing work-related stress, depression or anxiety were

- Workload pressures, including scheduling and shift work
- Interpersonal relationships, including difficulties with superiors, bullying or harassment
- Changes in the workplace, including reductions in resources, staffing levels and additional responsibilities for staff

Does all of this sound familiar to you? With an increasingly competitive global economy, it's a fairly safe bet that stress in the workplace will be with us for the foreseeable future. But what exactly is *work-related stress*? The HSE defines it as 'a harmful reaction that people have to undue pressures and demands placed upon them at work'.

I want you to pay particular attention to one word in the above sentence: *reaction*. You could survey a hundred different people who had exactly the same pressures and demands placed upon them and all of them could *react* in different ways depending on how they *thought* about their particular situation. Controversially, the psychologist Graham Price (2013) asserts that British adults are experiencing higher levels of stress than their grandparents, who had bombs rained upon them in the Blitz during the Second World War, and attributes this tendency to modern-day self-obsession rather than 'grit' and 'Dunkirk spirit'. Angela Patmore, author of *The Truth About Stress* (2006), suggests that the condition has given rise to a multi-billion pound and dollar industry dedicated to curing people of this new modern 'disease', and finds this approach very dubious.

Whether or not you subscribe to Price and Patmore's views on stress, it's worth reflecting on the subjective nature of this condition. Stress is a reaction to an *external event*, something that happens to us in the workplace or elsewhere. The way we *think* about this event will largely determine how we *feel* and *act* in response to the stressor: anxious and avoidant or excited and galvanised into action. Let's look at an example.

It's presentation time!

Jacqui and Kalpana are employed as chartered accountants for a large multimedia company in central London. Their line manager, Jack, has assigned them both the task of giving a 20 minute presentation at the next company board meeting on their analysis of the organisation's auditing procedures and recommendations for improvement. From Kalpana's perspective this is a fantastic opportunity to raise her profile within the senior management team and she feels excited at the prospect of giving the presentation. She thinks, 'This is great – it's the chance I've been longing for. I'll show Jack and the SMT what I'm capable of with my analysis and recommendations – that's bound to improve my chances of getting a promotion at my next appraisal.' Jacqui responds to Jack's request in a completely different way: she's absolutely terrified at the prospect of giving a presentation in front of her boss and the SMT. She's thinking, 'I'm going to be in the spotlight for 20 minutes! I'm bound to get nervous and they'll all see it. What if I blush and dry up during the presentation? They'll realise that I'm out of my depth and have been promoted above my level of competence within the department.'

Jacqui and Kalpana have the same job within the organisation and have been called upon to perform the same task. The key difference between them is the way in which they separately perceive the task and experience the subsequent emotional consequences.

You can use the **ABC model** as a highly effective stress-busting tool whenever you encounter challenges in the workplace that take you outside of your comfort zone. The model will help you to reframe what you perceive to be potentially stressful situations and transform them into opportunities for personal growth and advancement. Let's apply the model to Jacqui's situation.

Reframing the presentation

A = Activating event or adversity: Jacqui has been given the task of presenting her review of the company's auditing procedures at the next board meeting.

B = Beliefs/thoughts: Jacqui is thinking, 'I'm bound to get nervous and they'll all see it. They'll realise that I'm out of my depth and have been promoted above my level of competence within the department.'

C = Consequences (emotional, behavioural, physiological): Jacqui is feeling increasingly anxious as the week of the presentation looms closer and she is repeatedly running negative scenarios in her head. Increased anxiety is distracting Jacqui from preparing for the presentation. In fact, she has become *avoidant* because any reminder of the task causes an increase in anxiety. Constant worry about the presentation outside of work has also led to an increase in adrenaline when Jacqui should be relaxing and is wreaking havoc with her sleeping patterns so that her energy levels are depleted.

D = Disputing: Jacqui remembers the ABC model and engages her rational, left prefrontal cortex in analysing the situation objectively. This immediately soothes her emotionally overactive right prefrontal cortex and gives her some respite. She challenges her negative assumptions about the situation and figures that her boss, Jack, has asked her to give the presentation because he has every confidence in her professional abilities – he wouldn't want her performance to reflect badly on him. She also *normalises* her feelings of nervousness about the forthcoming presentation and concludes that, as public speaking is one of the most common fears worldwide, the majority of her colleagues would experience 'butterflies' in the same situation and will empathise if she seems nervous to start with.

E = Effective new thinking: Having vigorously attacked her negative thoughts, Jacqui is able to replace them with a more helpful outlook concerning the forthcoming presentation. She has reframed this potentially stressful threat as an opportunity to shine in front of board members and increase her standing within the organisation. She accepts that some feelings of nervousness before and during the presentation are inevitable, but they're not a danger signal that she will fall apart. She remembers that a helpful strategy to counter future worry is to bring her focus of attention back to the present by concentrating on preparing for the presentation. Her feelings of anxiety begin to decline and she experiences a newfound sense of confidence and purpose.

As I mentioned above, the process of *disputing* your unhelpful negative thoughts engages your rational left prefrontal cortex and gives you some respite from the right prefrontal cortex, which has stronger links with the stormy, emotion-generating subcortical areas of the brain (Siegel, 2013). It's sometimes helpful to verbalise your specific worries about a situation and get them down on paper rather than experience them randomly whizzing around your head. That way you can launch a counter-attack against each of these unhelpful thoughts. A useful tool to add to your stress-busting arsenal is the **SIT-SOT model.**

The SIT-SOT model

SITs = Stress Increasing Thoughts: These types of thoughts tend to focus on hypothetical 'what if' types of worry about a situation and magnify any negative aspects of the challenge so that they can seem overwhelming. They can be distorted and influenced by *emotional reasoning* – looking at the situation through the lens of your anxiety. These thoughts need to be counterbalanced with SOTs.

SOTs = Stress Overcoming Thoughts: These thoughts offer a more rational ('left-brain') appraisal of the situation rather than a purely emotional response. They are realistic, problem solving in focus and enable you to access your resources for dealing with the challenge in question.

Using the SIT-SOT model involves the following steps:

1   Briefly describe the stressful situation as you perceive it.
2   Describe any negative thoughts you may have about the situation that are causing you to experience anxiety (or any other unhelpful negative emotion). Record these in the left-hand column of the SIT-SOT form (available at Appendix 6).
3   For each stress increasing thought recorded in the left-hand column, counter with a stress overcoming thought in the right-hand column. Wherever possible, try to give these responses a problem solving focus.

Table 4.1 is an example of a completed SIT-SOT sheet constructed to help Jacqui deal with her stressful situation.

Hopefully, you can see from this table that the SIT-SOT model can help you to meet potentially stressful situations head on and tackle them through a problem solving approach. Undertaking this process also weakens unhelpful thoughts and deprives them of their ability to disturb you.

Table 4.1 Jacqui's SIT-SOT analysis

Stressful situation: giving a presentation to SMT	
Stress Increasing Thoughts (SITs)	**Stress Overcoming Thoughts (SOTs)**
1 My face will go red and everyone will see that I'm anxious.	1 Even if my face goes red, people watching won't necessarily think that I'm anxious. I've seen people who've looked flushed whilst giving a presentation but haven't given it a second thought.
2 Anxiety will overwhelm me and my mind will go blank during the presentation.	2 I'm bound to feel a bit nervous at the start of the presentation—most people would be. But if I memorise the introductory part of the presentation, I won't have to worry about drying up and I'll soon hit my stride.
3 One of the board members might ask me an awkward question that I won't be able to answer.	3 If I spend my time preparing thoroughly rather than worrying, I'll know more about the subject than anyone there. Even if someone throws me a 'curve ball', I'll handle it as best as I can. I could also offer to send out additional information with the minutes of the meeting.
4 Kalpana is presenting before me. She's bound to give a good performance and I'll look shaky in comparison.	4 My presentational style is just different to Kalpana's. I know that a number of the board members are highly analytical and will like my attention to detail and objectivity.

Tolerating uncertainty in an uncertain world

The situation confronting Jacqui is an example of a known challenge that will occur at a specific time (e.g. giving the presentation to board members). But many people experience stress in the workplace by worrying about a range of things that *might* happen, even if there is very little likelihood of the feared event occurring. For these individuals, a thought challenging approach such as the SIT-SOT model offers little comfort, as once you have dealt with one worrying thought, another springs up to take its place. This is similar to the many-headed hydra of Lerna in Greek mythology, who was eventually slain by Hercules. Any attempt to cut off one of its heads resulted in the poisonous serpent growing another two heads and becoming even more lethal.

If Jacqui were inclined toward this kind of intolerance of uncertainty, countering the worrying thought that she may go blank during the presentation with the reassurance that she could memorise the first few lines might give rise to a subsequent (albeit unlikely) anxiety that her laptop may fail. Even if she considered bringing two laptops to counter this risk, she might then think about the possibility of the projector breaking down. The point is that if someone suffers from an intolerance of uncertainty, no amount of reassurance will help them to rationalise the *unlikelihood* of the feared event happening (Dugas & Robichaud, 2007) because they'll still worry about this minute possibility ('Even if the chance of the plane crashing is three million to one, what if I'm sitting on *that* plane?'). Even if they are able to resolve one worrying thought, it will be quickly replaced by another, and then another, spiralling into a succession of 'worry chains'. If you can identify with this style of worrying, you're not alone. *Everyone* worries – some individuals more than others—but if you're constantly plagued by the possibility of negative things happening that are outside your sphere of control, you are probably experiencing high levels of stress in the workplace (and possibly outside of it) and could benefit from a different approach to dealing with uncertainty.

Question your beliefs about worry

Strange though it may seem, you may hold *positive* beliefs about worrying without even knowing it. These positive beliefs about the benefits of worry generally fall into five categories (Dugas and Robichaud, 2007) so it's worth considering whether you endorse any of them.

1   Worrying helps me to solve problems

People who hold this type of belief think that worrying will help them to figure out the best solution for a challenge they are facing or even pre-empt a negative outcome by considering different scenarios and how they can be dealt with effectively. This process often gets mistaken for *problem solving*, which I'll come to later. The big difference is that problem solving is a rational, 'left-brain' activity whereas worry fires up the *fight or flight* threat response, making clear thinking difficult. It also inclines us toward *emotional reasoning* so that we're more likely to see dangers where they don't exist.

2   Worrying motivates me and pushes me to achieve

In this example, worry is seen as a spur to action driving the individual on to accomplish their goal. If we take Jacqui's example of anticipating a forthcoming presentation, she may think that worrying about the future event will galvanise her into preparing an excellent piece of work. But as we've seen, worrying about the presentation can lead to procrastination because any reminder of the task ahead fills her with anxiety and she becomes avoidant rather than task focussed.

3   Worrying will help me to prepare for the worst

This is the belief that if you endure the 'pain' in advance by worrying, it will somehow fortify you for a negative outcome. However, imagining the worst that can happen will give you a *negative bias* of the future event and deplete your resources so that you will be less able to rise to the challenge. Worrying, like any other cognitively demanding activity, severely depletes glucose levels in the brain and thus mental and physical energy.

4   Worrying stops bad things from happening to me

This is an insidious belief and is similar to superstitious thinking in that the person believes that the very act of worrying will ward off misfortune. Similar to this is a type of existential fear that, 'if I stop worrying, it will tempt fate.' The problem with this type of belief is that it becomes unconsciously reinforced every time the person worries and nothing bad happens. So if Jacqui worries constantly and the presentation goes well in spite of this, she may believe at some level that her worrying had magically prevented failure rather than attributing the success of the event to her own skills. People who slip into this type of belief find themselves in a constant state of worry trying to prevent any number of bad things from happening in an uncertain world.

5   Worrying means that I'm conscientious about my job

Some individuals openly display their worry as a badge of honour implying that they care deeply about the responsibilities placed upon them. In some instances worry and stress are almost deemed to be status symbols: 'I worry about my work because it's so important'. But worry is a chosen *response* to stress and a pretty dysfunctional one. Maintaining clear thinking, mental focus and practising appropriate self-care are greater signs of conscientiousness.

Increase your tolerance of uncertainty

Benjamin Franklin famously said that there are only two things in life of which we can be certain: death and taxes. We live in an increasingly complex and uncertain world where the pace of change is more rapid as a consequence of globalisation and advances in technology. There are very few 'jobs for life' as in previous generations and uncertainty in the workplace is a reality that many people have to accept as part of their career. It's hardly surprising that many people use worry as a default strategy when faced with so much uncertainty but, as we've seen, worrying excessively is an unhelpful process as it wastes mental and physical energy, reduces self-confidence and can make life feel joyless. So how can you banish worry from your life? There are two possibilities. The first one is that *you can do everything in your power to make certain that nothing bad will happen in your life.* If you are one of life's worriers, chances are that you have already tried this strategy. The question you need to ask yourself is, has this strategy worked? If you still worry and suffer from anxiety it would suggest that the answer is 'no'. The only other possibility is to *increase your tolerance of uncertainty.*

This may seem like a daunting prospect because of the potential discomfort involved, but if you think about it, deliberately going outside of your comfort zone and gaining self-confidence is infinitely preferable to a life of worry. It will also give you back control over your anxiety levels in response to stress. Every time you place yourself in an uncertain situation and tolerate the anxiety, you will inoculate yourself against future stressful events. The trick is to start small and build up your tolerance of uncertainty gradually. For example:

Send text messages without checking for errors

↓

Send low importance emails without checking for errors

↓

Permanently delete emails and avoid keeping them 'in case' you need them

↓

Speak up at meetings without mentally preparing what you are going to say

↓

Don't obtain opinions from others before you make minor decisions

↓

Once you have made a decision, move on without considering whether you could have done better

Remember Seligman's example of 'psychological capital' that we considered in the previous chapter: every time you engage with a challenge that takes you outside of your comfort zone, you make a *deposit* and add to your resilience capital. You will also find that the more you engage in an activity that you usually find anxiety provoking, the less anxious you will be next time you engage in that activity. Let's examine how this principle has worked for Jacqui.

Throughout her professional life Jacqui has suffered from a fear of public speaking and her nightmare scenario is giving a presentation in front of senior managers. She has developed a number of strategies to avoid giving presentations, including taking sick leave on the day of the presentation. Each time Jacqui avoids giving a presentation, she experiences a temporary feeling of relief and her anxiety subsides (Figure 4.1). The problem with this pattern of behaviour is that Jacqui's respite from anxiety is only temporary and next time she is called upon to speak in public her fear reasserts itself. She maintains her fear of public speaking because with each escape, she has taught herself that she has avoided a catastrophe: she never learns that her greatest nightmare – drying up in front of the audience, will not occur and that she is quite capable of delivering a reasonable presentation.

Jacqui has decided that she can no longer hide anymore. If she wants to progress in her career, she will have to deliver presentations as part of her role and overcome her fear of public speaking. Jacqui grasps her courage with both hands and delivers the presentation to the board. In this instance, she stays in the situation and learns something very important. *If you stay in a feared situation long enough, your anxiety can't get any greater and will start to come down* (Figure 4.2). Your brain then registers a key message – nothing bad is happening here!

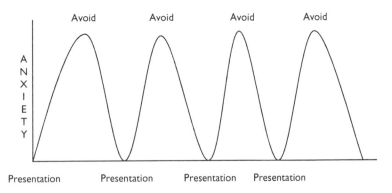

Figure 4.1 Jacqui's avoidance pattern.

Having successfully delivered the presentation to the board, Jacqui experiences a newfound confidence and agrees to present on a monthly basis. When the next board meeting comes around, Jacqui still experiences quite high levels of anxiety but not as intense as the previous occasion. She grits her teeth and sees the task through. Jacqui notices that not only did she not experience as much anxiety as the first time she presented, her feelings of anxiety also fade away quicker. Each time Jacqui gives a presentation, her level of anxiety decreases along with the amount of time it takes her to recover (Figure 4.3).

Now it's your turn! Think of an activity that you have been avoiding because it makes you anxious, but that would be of benefit if you carried it out. What I'm asking you to do is set up what we CBT therapists call a *behavioural experiment* so that you can directly confront the situation that makes you anxious and learn from it. These are the key steps you need to undertake:

1   Describe the situation that makes you anxious.
2   Predict *exactly* what you think will happen.
3   Describe how you would know it had happened, *objectively speaking.*
4   Rate your strength of conviction about your fear coming true on a scale between 0 – 100%.
5   Describe what you will do to test your prediction. Identify and drop any safety behaviours.

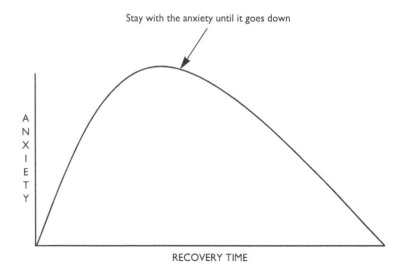

Figure 4.2 Anxiety exposure curve.

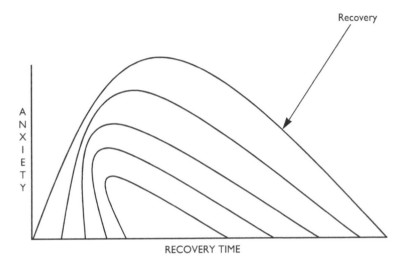

Figure 4.3 Repeated exposure pattern.

After your experiment, ask yourself:

1   What actually happened in the situation? Did my fear come true?
2   What have I learned from this experiment? How strong is my con-
    viction that my fear will come true in a similar situation, on a scale
    between 0 – 100%?
3   What else can I do to test my original prediction? (if your rating
    hasn't dropped to 0%)

Table 4.2 shows an example of how Jacqui set up her behavioural experiment before giving the presentation.

   When you carry out your behavioural experiment, there are a couple
of important points I'd like you to bear in mind. It's important to *operationalise* your predictions and make them as objectively measurable as
possible. For example, it would be of no use whatsoever if Jacqui's prediction was that the board members would *think* she was nervous whilst
giving her presentation – that would be an *inference*. She would need to
operationalise this prediction by determining the evidence for this that
she could objectively observe – that one or more of the board members
would *comment* on her nervousness.

   Remember what I said earlier in this chapter about the role of *safety
behaviours* in maintaining and contributing to your anxiety. In previous

Table 4.2 Jacqui's behavioural experiment

Describe the situation	Predict *exactly* what you think will happen. How will you know? Rate your conviction 0–100%	What will you do to test your prediction? Identify and ban safety behaviours	What actually happened? Did my fear come true?	What have I learned? How likely is my fear to come true in a similar situation? (0–100%)
Giving a presentation at the board meeting	People at the meeting will notice that I'm nervous. I'll know because someone will comment on it (80%).	I'll go ahead and give the presentation without making excuses. I normally avoid eye contact and hide behind the lap top and projector. This time I'll make eye contact with everyone and stand up during the presentation.	I felt very anxious at the start of the presentation but I focused on the task and my nerves gradually subsided. I made good eye contact and moved around during the presentation. No one commented on my nervousness.	I've learned that my nerves are high at the start of the presentation but I can handle it. My anxiety level declines quickly if I focus on the task in hand. My prediction for similar situations is around 20%. I'll take every opportunity to present in front of senior staff

situations when Jacqui couldn't get out of giving a presentation, she would avoid making eye contact with her audience and hide behind props, a lectern, her laptop, the projector – anything! This behaviour sent a message to her brain that the situation was dangerous (because she was trying to hide) and triggered an increase in anxiety. And after the event it strengthened Jacqui's unconscious belief that if she *hadn't* hidden from the audience and *had* made eye contact, she'd have fallen apart. By consciously identifying and dropping her safety behaviours, Jacqui is able to *disconfirm* her belief that something bad will happen if she doesn't try to 'protect' herself.

You can set up your own stress-busting behavioural experiments by using the form at Appendix 7.

Don't worry – get busy!

We've talked about the way in which *hypothetical*, 'what if' type of worry can contribute to your stress levels and that the best way of dealing with it is to increase your tolerance of uncertainty. But what about actual problems that are confronting you and causing you stress? Well done for differentiating between the two. Broadly speaking, Table 4.3 shows the two types of worry and two different strategies for dealing with them in CBT.

Hopefully I've given you enough ammunition to deal with hypothetical worry. I will now turn my attention to helping you deal more effectively with actual problems.

The first thing to say is that as well as worrying, *everyone* experiences problems throughout their life. What makes a big difference in terms of how much anxiety people experience is their *attitude* to actual problems and their strategies for dealing with them. Research tells us that people who worry excessively are just as effective at solving problems as anyone else (Dugas and Robichaud, 2007). However, they have what is described in psychological terms as a *negative problem orientation*. This means that when confronted with a problem in life, these individuals have a tendency to regard the problem as threatening. They also don't have much confidence in their capability to solve problems, even if they've successfully dealt with similar problems in the past. Remember what we discussed about *negative filters*: they only recall failures and filter out successes to strengthen their negative beliefs. These people also think that if they attempt to solve the problem, it will inevitably turn out badly. All of this negative thinking triggers anxiety and increases their stress levels. Because they find the prospect of tackling the problem so aversive, these unfortunate individuals often postpone dealing with the problem because of the anxiety it causes them. Unfortunately, this procrastination usually results in an even bigger, more complicated problem.

Table 4.3 Two types of worry

Type of worry	Strategy
1 Hypothetical ('what if') worry	Increasing tolerance of anxiety
2 Actual problems	Active problem solving

The best way to deal with any challenge that you encounter is to engage in active problem solving using the steps outlined next.

Stage 1: Describe the problem as clearly as possible

You need to be very specific in defining the problem you intend to solve. Getting this stage right is critical because a vaguely defined problem will undermine any potential strategies for solving it. The problem also needs to be within your direct control to some extent. If the problem is completely outside your control it can usually be categorised as a *hypothetical worry* ('what if?') and you would be best advised to use the strategies outlined for increasing tolerance of uncertainty. Let's go back to Frank, whom you may recall is having a challenging time settling into his new role. He has taken over a new team and Frank quickly gets the sense that they really liked his predecessor and are noticeably unenthusiastic about his appointment as their manager. One of the team had also competed unsuccessfully against Frank for his current role and has exhibited slightly challenging behaviours in meetings since his appointment. Frank's initial assessment of his problem was 'My new team are being a pain in the a**e!', which, although a heartfelt expression of his problem, is definitely not specific. After some reflection, Frank reformulates the problem as 'I need to improve the relationship between me and my new team.'

You will notice that Frank has some control over the situation as far as this goal is concerned; he is, after all, their manager and has a certain amount of influence. If, on the other hand, Frank had a tyrannical boss who was impervious to influence but he needed to stay in the job, Frank's goal might be more suited to emotional regulation than practical problem solving (e.g. 'challenge my thinking and reduce my stress level in reaction to my boss' unreasonable behaviour.')

Stage 2: Develop as many strategic options as you can to solve the problem

You've probably sat in on a number of meetings where someone has facilitated a 'brainstorming' session: everyone contributes ideas, the facilitator notes them on a flip chart and eventually the group selects the best solution. This method probably seems like something of a cliché now, a scene from the popular TV comedy *The Office* with Ricky Gervais. Strangely, given that this is such a frequently used approach, most people struggle to generate a wide range of potential solutions to their problems when left to their own devices. Dugas and Robichaud (2007) noted that this is probably due to the fact that we adhere to habit, defaulting to previously used solutions to solve our problems. This is similar to Daniel Kahneman's (2011) notion that we are hard-wired to engage in mental shortcuts (heuristics) or what he described as *system 1 thinking*.

It's usually helpful to engage in problem solving with other people, as they may be able to consider your challenge objectively and offer different perspectives to the tried and tested 'shortcuts' that you have previously used. If you have to solve the problem alone, give yourself the best chance by going about the task as *creatively* as possible. First, engage in a free-flow of potential solutions, noting them all down without considering whether they seem stupid or impractical. Avoid any inclination to self-censor. This is what Alex Faikney Osborn, the original inventor of 'brainstorming', referred to as the *deferment of judgement principle* (2011). You can always sift out the more outlandish ideas after you have gone through this process. You need to reduce your inhibitions and tap into your creative thought processes. On this occasion you are trying to engage your more emotionally sensitive right prefrontal cortex rather than your logical (and perhaps slightly inhibiting) left prefrontal cortex. This is why people in creative industries often report using alcohol to stimulate their creative resources (Andrew et al., 2012), although I definitely wouldn't advocate that approach! If you get stuck at this point it could be because you are too close to the problem emotionally and it might be helpful to de-centre. You can do this by engaging in a technique called 'best friend's argument'. Take a moment to stand back from the situation and imagine you are helping a friend to deal with the same problem. What advice would you give them? Make a note of any new insights. You may have noticed from past experience that it's much easier to help other people solve their problems than it is to come up with solutions for challenges that you have to deal with. This is because we find it difficult to be objective about our own circumstances. The 'best friend' technique helps you to break out of your often narrow focus and see the problem from another perspective.

Stage 3: Explore the advantages and disadvantages for each potential solution and score them according to difficulty and usefulness

This process is similar to the one I outlined in carrying out a *cost and benefit analysis* (CBA) in Chapter 3. The difference is that the CBA is technique aimed at helping you to work through any *ambivalence* you may be experiencing at the prospect of contemplating a course of action. With active problem solving your aim is to rate each potential solution according to its level of *difficulty* or *usefulness* on a scale of 0–5.

Stage 4: Choose the 'best fit' strategic option

Having carried out the above rating process, you will hopefully be in a better position to choose a serviceable strategy from the various options you have considered. It's at this point that you need to go for the 'best fit' strategy even if it doesn't *feel* like the ideal solution (it probably won't). The essence of decision making is to work within the information available and take action within a time frame *even if the potential solution does not seem perfect*. Failure to do so leads to procrastination (usually due to low tolerance of uncertainty) and a *paralysis of analysis* – getting sidetracked into constantly seeking more information and putting off taking action.

Stage 5: Break down your 'best fit' strategy into individual steps

This part of your problem solving strategy is vitally important because if you don't break the actions down into clear, manageable steps, you risk being overwhelmed by the task. Now might be a good time to review the section on constructing SMART goals in Chapter 3 (Specific, Measurable, Achievable, Realistic, Time bound). It will also be helpful for you to identify any potential challenges that may occur when carrying out these actions and consider contingency plans for dealing with them. Although it may seem counterintuitive to think of potential obstacles when you're trying to get yourself motivated, it's far better to foresee them while you're in a calm state of mind rather than when you experience a 'bump in the road' along the way and start to feel the pressure. Russian General Alexander Suvorov remained undefeated after sixty battles and adopted the strategy of 'train hard, fight easy'. You could adopt a similar approach to dealing with your challenges by adopting the maxim 'prepare hard, fight easy'.

Stage 6: Execute and evaluate

You need to avoid too much deliberation and take action as soon as you have a best fit strategy in order to prevent yourself from procrastination. The initial first steps of putting your plans into action may require some psychological effort, particularly if the potential outcome is important to you. You need to remind yourself that avoidance of action will only make the challenge you are facing more difficult to tackle in the long run. If you've ever swum in the sea, it's a bit like taking the first plunge when you have to brace yourself against the initial chill of the water. If you persevere for a few moments, it becomes a pleasurable, invigorating experience.

You also need to develop an objective set of measures for determining whether or not your chosen strategy is effective. This is important because you want to avoid expending vital time and energy on a less than optimum course of action. You may resort to another of the potential strategic options that you came up with at Stage 2. Also, setting up a mechanism for evaluating your strategy to some extent takes the emotional sting of uncertainty out of embarking on a course of action. As I mentioned previously, we often find it difficult to tolerate uncertainty, particularly when there's a lot at stake (emotionally, financially and materially). Setting out on a blind path will inevitably raise your anxiety levels, but knowing that you have a means of assessing progress and readjusting your course will increase confidence in your chosen strategic option. Important questions to consider as part of your evaluation include:

- To what extent has the problem been solved?
- What else needs to be done to resolve any remaining aspects of the problem?
- What changes do I need to make to my chosen strategy or do I need to try another strategic option?
- What have I learned from carrying out my strategic option?
- How can I use this learning to deal more effectively with other problems I may encounter?

The last question is important and it's worth making the effort of recording any lessons learned, as this will increase your problem solving ability *and* your tolerance of uncertainty.

Let's go back to Frank to see how he applies the above process to his particular problem. Fortunately, he is able to re-establish contact with James, an executive coach who used to mentor him in his previous role. They meet at James' office and he helps Frank to deal with his current challenge by teaching him the problem solving skills that we have just reviewed.

James: It's been a while since we last met. How's the new job going – are you pleased you made the move?

Frank: If I'm honest, I'm having second thoughts about the whole thing and I feel a bit out of my depth.

James: Why's that? You've always struck me as very capable and, in my opinion, I thought you'd outgrown your previous role – you were stagnating.

Frank: The point is, I didn't anticipate taking over such a hostile team. I feel as though I'm on the back foot all of the time and my self-confidence has been completely eroded.

James: What's so bad about this particular team?

Frank: I get the sense that they really liked the manager I took over from and to make things worse, one of the guys in the team went for my job and didn't get it. He's a real thorn in my side and openly challenges my decisions in meetings. The rest of the team often follow his lead or just seem sullen and unenthusiastic.

James: Sounds as though you're encountering what Bruce Tuckman (1965) described as the normal stages of group development: forming, storming, norming and performing.

Frank: What's that all about?

James: Tuckman reckoned that when groups come together, they have to go through some initial turbulence until each member settles into their role. You're the new boss and your introduction has changed the group dynamic so you've triggered off this process to some extent.

Frank: So what can I do about it?

James: You want to get through the 'storming' part as swiftly as possible, get them into 'norming', gelling as a team with you as their new manager and then, hopefully, into 'performing'.

Frank: I'm not sure I know where to start in spite of what you've taught me.

James: The first thing I'd advise you to do is stand back from the situation and get a more detached and less emotional perspective. I suggest you adopt a problem solving approach and break the challenge down into manageable steps.

Frank: OK, I'm willing to try that. How do you suggest I start?

James: You need to be very specific about what the actual problem is. At the moment you've described it in terms of having a hostile team and feeling a lack of self-confidence. As far as the team's concerned, what's within your direct control?

Frank: Well, although I'm in charge, I can't force them to like me. As long as they're fulfilling their basic obligations, I've got no grounds for complaint.

James: So if you can't force them to like you but you want to improve your standing with the team, what's the one area you can influence?

Frank: My relationship with them I guess.

James: So how would you define the problem specifically?

Frank: 'I need to improve the relationship between me and my new team'.

James: Excellent. (notes problem on the whiteboard)

PROBLEM: Improve relationship between me and new team

James: So the next step is for you to generate a number of potential solutions for solving this particular problem.

Frank: That's where I get stuck. I keep thinking of different ways to tackle the problem but that just triggers another set of worries about what might go wrong.

James: You're having trouble de-centring from the problem. You used to mentor staff in your previous job. If one of your mentees came to you and said they were having trouble developing a positive relationship with their new team, what would you advise them to do?

Frank: Now you come to mention it, I remember advising someone in a similar situation to invite the team out for a drink to get to know them socially. But that probably won't work because they're such a miserable bunch.

James: Let's jot down the ideas first. If you keep censoring yourself, you'll remain stuck. What other ideas would you suggest?

Frank: I guess I could take the guy who didn't get my job to one side and have an open and honest discussion with him.

James: Yes, find out what his agenda is and see if you can work out an arrangement that would be mutually beneficial. Go on.

Frank: I could take them all paintballing – probably a bit '80s.

James: Let's describe that as 'team building away day' and worry about the detail later.

Frank: I've thought about going on the attack and telling them all that I've noticed their lack of enthusiasm and that they need to draw a line under their old boss leaving and move on.

James: OK, let's get that down. Anything else?

Frank: Meet with them individually to find out exactly how they feel about their role and any grievances they may have.

James: Interesting. You could treat it like an informal evaluation, get some consensus and make suggestions for improvement at the next meeting. Any other ideas?

Frank: That's pretty much all I can come up with at the moment.

Table 4.4 Frank's problem solving strategy

Strategy	Advantages	Disadvantages	Difficulty (0–5)	Usefulness (0–5)
Take the team out for a drink and get to know them socially	The informal setting might lead to a friendlier interaction with team members	Might give the more negative members of the team a chance to be critical in a social situation Team members might refuse to participate	4	2
Meet with obstructive team member and have an open discussion	Meeting separately would prevent any negativity contaminating the team	The member of staff could tell other team members he was being victimised for his honesty	1	1
Arrange team building away day	It would offer an opportunity for bonding A different environment might lead to a more positive dynamic within the team	Members of the team might see it as a predictable attempt to bond with them and indicate a lack of confidence Senior manager might not agree to funding for the away day due to cut-backs	4	3
Assert myself with the team and draw attention to their shortcomings	This would finally clear the air and show the team who's boss	Could lead to further resentment and team adopting a passive-aggressive stance If the attempt fails, it would weaken authority within the team	2	1
Meet with each team member individually and discuss their role	Meeting separately would prevent any negativity contaminating the team The context of the meeting would be neutral and could facilitate an open discussion An opportunity to get to know each team member better	Would require an additional investment of time during a very busy period	2	5

James: That's not bad going. You've moved from no ideas at all to five potential solutions. The next stage is for us to review each of these ideas and consider any potential advantages or disadvantages if you carried them out. We also need to rate how difficult they would be for you to carry out in practical terms and also how useful they would be in terms of achieving your goal. What do you think?

Frank: It's definitely worth a try.

After further discussion with James, Frank managed to carry out a detailed evaluation of each potential strategy as set out in Table 4.4.

After reflection, Frank decides that meeting each team member individually offers the best strategy under the circumstances. It will give him the opportunity to get to know them outside of a group setting and hopefully lead to a more positive interpersonal dynamic. Although it will require a considerable investment of his time within a hectic work schedule, Frank figures that team members will appreciate the effort he is taking to get to know them. He quickly dismisses the idea of confronting the recalcitrant member of the team on his own realising that this would give him even more ammunition to criticise Frank amongst his colleagues. Similarly, he rejects 'laying down the law' with the team as far too authoritarian and almost guaranteed to breed further resentment. The idea of inviting the team for a drink seemed to offer a positive gesture until Frank considered the risk that alcohol might disinhibit certain individuals and offer them the opportunity to criticise him outside of the workplace. It might be better to save the social invitation until he gets to know the team better. Arranging a team building event came a close second as a potential strategy and Frank thought he might return to it if meeting with team members individually didn't yield the results he was hoping for.

Frank decides to evaluate the success of his chosen strategy by asking each team member to rate their current level of job satisfaction at the meeting and then subsequently at a further individual review in 2 months. As well as providing him with a measurable means of evaluating the effectiveness of his chosen strategy, Frank considers that this method will send out a strong message to team members that he takes their well-being seriously and intends to make positive changes on their behalf. It also provides an opportunity for team members to *specify* areas of discontent so that Frank can take action and cut through any lingering resentment within the team. If this strategy works, Frank will note what he has learned on this occasion and draw on this knowledge if he encounters similar challenges in his career.

Now it's your turn. Think of an issue that you've been struggling with and tackle it using this problem solving process. You can find a problem solving strategy evaluation worksheet at Appendix 8.

Now that you've got a number of tools for dealing with stress at work, I'd like to introduce you to a range of techniques that will boost your self-confidence.

Create a super-confident you

Very often within CBT, it is helpful to equip clients with various emotional and psychological resources that will enable them to meet different challenges in their lives. This process is called *resource development and installation* (Shapiro, 2001) and it can work for you. If you want to become super-confident in certain situations *at will*, you can create this state of mind and the positive feelings that accompany it in a number of ways.

1   Your personal history

Find somewhere quiet to sit and close your eyes. Think of a time when you felt totally confident and unstoppable. Revisit that event in your mind as though it is taking place again *right now*. What can you see? Pay attention to what is happening around you, particularly images and colours. What can you hear? What sounds do you notice – where are they coming from? What can you feel? Tune into any physical sensations that feel positive and empowering and notice in particular how you are moving and what posture you have adopted. Do you notice any pleasant fragrances or even flavours that are associated with the event and make you feel good?

Now, *totally immerse yourself* in this experience; pay particular attention to any feelings of confidence and focus on these sensations in your body. What *word* or *brief sentence* would conjure up this powerful memory and the accompanying feelings of confidence for you (e.g. 'unstoppable')? Make a note of this word – you can use it as a *trigger* to access powerful feelings of confidence associated with this memory whenever you want.

2   Other people

Even if you can't recall a time when you felt highly confident, you can get yourself into this state of mind by drawing on positive role models. Think of someone you admire who acts in a confident manner that you would like to emulate. It could be anyone: a friend or work colleague, someone in the media, even a character from a film or book (James Bond or Wonder Woman, for example). Don't inhibit your imagination. It may seem like fantasising, but this exercise has a serious purpose: to enable you to access positive and empowering emotions.

Once you have chosen your role model, *imagine yourself acting like them*. What posture would they adopt and how would they move? How would they talk in a confident manner? How would they think and act? Immerse yourself in the experience of inhabiting this new role and pay attention to any feelings of confidence that arise in your body when you think and act in this way.

3   Symbols of confidence

Any image that provides you with a feeling of confidence can be used in this way. For example, clients I have worked with derive confidence in challenging situations from the image of a mountain or tree. They imagine themselves as embodying the positive qualities of these natural phenomena such as strength and gravitas. Another fantastic resource for generating confidence and other positive emotions is *music*. Years ago, I worked with a therapist whose wife was coaching a world famous boxer in psychological motivation. The boxer would draw on previous positive memories until he felt supremely confident. At this point he would play Tina Turner's 'Simply the Best' to anchor that feeling of supreme confidence. Guess what music his promoters played when he entered the ring? You can use exactly the same technique and create your own super-confidence top 10 tunes.

Rehearse the new confident you dealing with future challenges

Now that you have a range of resources to draw on for developing a confident state of mind, it will be helpful to mentally rehearse using them in challenging situations to reinforce their potency. Think about a future situation that you anticipate will challenge you in some way. It's easy to identify this by simply noticing the type of emotion you feel when you think of this future event – for example, it may trigger feelings of anxiety, anger or shyness.

Find somewhere quiet, close your eyes and begin to 'play the film' of the future event in your imagination, making the rehearsal as vivid as possible by seeing, hearing, feeling and even smelling and tasting as part of this virtual reality experience. As the future event unfolds, notice any undesired emotions as they arise (e.g. anxiety, anger). At this point, bring your new resources into play.

Your history: Use your trigger word to evoke powerful feelings of confidence associated with previous situations when you had coped with adversity successfully. Remind yourself that you have the resources to cope with this particular challenge.

Other people: Evoke your positive role model and see them standing next to you offering encouragement ('we're going to do this thing together'). Draw strength from them and even feel yourself merging and becoming one with them.

Symbols of confidence: Call your power images to mind and feel yourself growing in confidence as you embody their qualities. Time to crank up your 'confidence power ballad'.

Notice feelings of strength and confidence spreading throughout your body and savour the feeling of being unstoppable. Now, imagine yourself dealing successfully with whatever is ebbing your confidence using the *freeze-frame technique*. Pause the whole situation while your draw on your resources for a further boost of confidence. When you feel ready, *unfreeze* the image and launch yourself back into the situation, confidently cutting through any remaining obstacles. You can repeat this process every time you encounter a new obstacle or if your confidence falters.

If you're sceptical about trying out this approach, remember what I said in Chapter 2 when we looked at mentally preparing for interviews. Neuroscience, cognitive science and sports psychology research suggests that positive imagery interventions have a powerful motivational effect and will give you the resources to deal with life challenges (Hackmann, Bennett-Levy and Holmes, 2011).

If I've managed to convince you so far, the final thing I'd like you to do is draw on these confidence building resources *prior to* and *during* the event you've been rehearsing. You could begin by selecting a future event that you anticipate finding *moderately* challenging and apply this new approach. Rate your confidence on a scale of 0 to 10 (10 being the highest score) before and after you activate your new resources. After you've tackled the challenge, review your performance and reflect on what you might have done differently when dealing with a similar situation in future. Above all, congratulate yourself for going outside of your comfort zone and build up a hierarchy of future challenges. In this way you will develop a virtuous cycle of facing up to challenges using your new resources, resulting in positive experiences that you can draw on when facing the next challenge.

If you put into practice what I've taught you so far in this chapter, you'll be able to handle stress and feel more confident. The final challenge we'll explore together is effective time management.

Manage your time at work

It's a well-known fact that British and American employees put in excessive hours within the workplace, often with severe consequences for their mental and physical well-being. This trend was explored in Madeline Bunting's study *Willing Slaves: How the Overwork Culture Is Ruling Our Lives* (2004) and a Health and Safety Laboratory Report published around the same time (HSL, 2003: 16) providing evidence of the link between increased working hours and poor psychological health. More recently, employees working excessive hours has led the Japanese government to plan the introduction of laws compelling workers to take annual leave due to an increase in *karoshi* – death through overwork (McCurry, 2015). In spite of Japan's intervention and the European working-time directive limit of 48 hours per week, the trend for working excessive hours seems set to continue within the context of an increasingly competitive global economy.

You may know friends and colleagues who regularly exceed their contracted hours but show no evidence of increased productivity and who may suffer the consequences such as mental stress and the strain placed on relationships with partners or families. If you notice this tendency in yourself, it's worth taking an honest look at what you're doing and asking yourself why you're doing it. Many people have developed unhelpful *beliefs* about how they should operate within the workplace. Perhaps the most common but misguided conviction is that you have to be *seen* to work hard and 'put in the hours' by managers and colleagues. This is often described as 'presenteeism', a term initially coined by psychology professor Cary Cooper, a leading expert in organisational management at Lancaster University Management School. It arises within the workplace when employees feel insecure, so they work increasingly longer hours to demonstrate their dedication to the job. If enough workers engage in this practice, it eventually becomes part of the organisation's culture. Unfortunately it has the opposite of the intended effect, in time leading to decreased productivity, burn out and deterioration in mental and physical well-being. In 2013 concerns were expressed within the media about the 'macho-hours' culture in London city banks after a young German intern, Moritz Erhadt, died after working until 6 am for three consecutive days at Bank of America Merrill Lynch (Gallagher, 2013). Erhadt's colleagues commented that long working hours were the norm within the investment banking sector due to the competitive nature of the work and 'pulling an all-nighter' was a rite of passage ritual for interns and other staff.

Even if you don't work in the frenetic environment of investment banking and there isn't the organisational culture of working 'macho hours', your own beliefs or work ethic could incline you to work longer then you need to for little gain. This happened to Natalie soon after she was promoted at work.

Natalie's treadmill

Natalie was delighted after being promoted to head of the human resources department within her company, but her euphoria soon wore off. She felt slightly insecure about her ability to do the new job and regularly stayed late until this routine became a dysfunctional habit. Natalie developed two unhelpful beliefs. First, that working longer

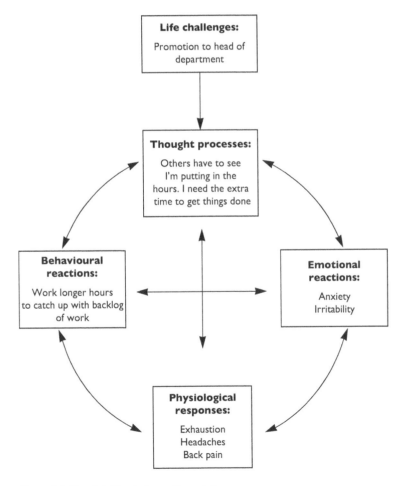

Figure 4.4 Natalie's life challenge formulation.

hours went with the seniority of her job and that her subordinates and manager must see evidence of this. Secondly, Natalie believed that she needed more time to get through the workload. Not only does Natalie get into the office early and leave late, she also takes home work at the weekend and fires off emails to colleagues so that they can see she's toiling away on Saturdays and Sundays. Understandably, this is having a detrimental effect on Natalie's relationship with her partner Chris as she has less time to spend with him and the children; she's also irritable and snappy a lot of the time. Her health has deteriorated too: she's developed problems sleeping, feels constantly exhausted and suffers from headaches and back pain – typical symptoms of stress. If only all of this sacrifice were worthwhile. But unfortunately, Natalie has driven herself into a vicious cycle of falling behind in her work during the day, because she's exhausted, then having to work late to catch up, and so on. If we formulate this situation within the context a life challenges model (Figure 4.4), it soon becomes apparent how this pattern of behaviour is maintaining itself.

If you find yourself falling into a similar dysfunctional vicious cycle of working excessively long hours and playing catch up, it's worth carrying out a life challenges formulation on your own patterns of behaviour and exploring some of the beliefs that might be driving your actions. Even if you are able to determine that you've drifted into an unhelpful routine, you may feel ambivalent about reducing the number of hours you are working, even if you can see the sense in doing so. This goes back to the difference between *intellectual insight* that we discussed in Chapter 1 and *emotional insight* – feeling that making positive changes would be the right decision for you. That's the time to do a cost and benefit analysis. It wasn't until Natalie did a CBA (Table 4.5) that she felt compelled to take positive action without any reservations.

This was the first time since she got the promotion that Natalie had given herself space to reflect and consider how her management of time at work had gotten out of hand and was having such a negative impact on herself and her family. Natalie's situation is typical of countless people I have treated for stress in my clinic. They very often have their nose too close to the grindstone to see how the problem they have created for themselves has become self-perpetuating. Gaining insight is a first step; perhaps you could also benefit from some self-reflection using these tools. However, insight alone won't help you to break out of this cycle. How do you cope with the demands of a modern career without putting in more hours? It's worth considering for a moment that even the prime minister of the UK and the president of

Table 4.5. Natalie's cost and benefit analysis

Costs and benefits of: working evening and weekends	
Costs (disadvantages)	*Benefits (advantages)*
Short-term	*Short-term*
For self	**For self**
I can't get a good night's sleep anymore	My boss and the staff I manage can
I keep getting headaches and back pain	see that I'm working hard
I drink wine every night to help	I'm keeping on top of the job
me relax	
I drink too much coffee during the day	
to stay alert	
I haven't got time to go to the gym or	
see friends	
For others	**For others**
Chris and the kids see much less of me	The increase in salary helped with
Chris thinks I'm permanently grumpy	the kids' school fees
I'm too stressed for sex	
Long-term	*Long-term*
For self	**For self**
I think my health will suffer if I carry on	I could go for a head of department
like this	job with another company in a
Lack of sleep will prematurely age me;	couple of years
I already look haggard	
I might develop a problem with alcohol	
dependency	
For others	**For others**
Chris and I might end up in couples	We might be able to pay off the
counselling at this rate	mortgage early
I'll miss the kids growing up	
People at work are getting pissed off	
with my bad moods	

the United States have just 24 hours a day at their disposal, the same as you and I, but with probably a much greater workload. You might suggest that sleeping less is an option, as Margaret Thatcher famously got by on four hours a night (Moore, 2014) but she was an exception. The British National Health Service (NHS, 2014) quotes 6 to 9 hours as the average amount of sleep required, depending on the individual. Anyway, her successor John Major slept eight hours a night – make of that what you will. Seriously though, putting in longer hours at work simply isn't a good long-term strategy, but *using your time as effectively as possible is.*

Making the most of your time at work

In *The 7 habits of highly effective people* (1999), Stephen Covey helpfully distinguishes four ways in which we tend to spend our time at work (and also outside work) engaging in activities according to their level of urgency and importance:

1   Urgent and important
2   Important but not urgent
3   Urgent but not important
4   Not important and not urgent

This is a very useful way of reviewing your patterns of behaviour within the workplace; I would like to emphasise *productivity* as a criterion and I'd encourage you to regard time and energy as precious, limited resources that require careful investment. Think about how you spend your time at work and consider which of the four modes described next typify the kind of activities you frequently engage in.

Mode 1: urgent and productive activities

In this situation you are usually under pressure to get things done as quickly as possible and can't put off the activity until later. There might be a sudden emergency that you have to deal with, like a complaint or a demand from senior management. Some type of deadline is looming or an unanticipated opportunity presents itself and you need to act swiftly to take advantage of it. We all encounter situations like this and the urgency required usually makes us highly productive: the adrenaline rush gives us added energy and the sense of immediacy provides added clarity and focus. Staying in this mode of behaviour is unsustainable in the long-term without experiencing burnout and a subsequent loss of productivity. However, many people get addicted to the buzz of urgency and unknowingly fall into dysfunctional patterns of behaviour that keep them locked into a punishing boom-and-bust cycle. You may have observed colleagues who procrastinate, putting off writing reports or preparing for important presentations until the last minute, when an approaching deadline galvanises them into action. Some individuals enjoy this sense of living on the edge and report that they find urgency energising. The problem with constantly operating in this mode is that it drains energy, leading to a loss of productivity during recovery time after a spike of frenetic activity.

Mode 2: urgent but unproductive activities

This description may appear contradictory at first glance, but we very often engage in activities that seem productive because of their sense of urgency. On closer examination you may find that these activities are urgent for other people and may distract you from your own priorities. Think of how many emails you receive marked 'urgent' and consider how often you have lost your focus of attention to read the content and possibly reply. Similar activities include interruptions and phone calls from colleagues requiring your urgent attention because they need to meet a deadline. Very often they are the 'firefighters' who find themselves stuck in Mode 1 and who cause disruption to those around them due to their lack of organisation. There will undoubtedly be exceptional circumstances in which you have to help colleagues to deal with an emergency, but it's worth considering how many of these demands on your precious time and energy could be deflected. As I will go on to explain in Chapter 5, maintaining your focus on a specific activity is vitally important if you want to optimise productivity and every interruption will cause you to lose momentum and energy. If you find it hard to say no to others, study the section on developing assertiveness skills in Chapter 6.

Mode 3: nonurgent and unproductive activities

As the title implies, this mode of behaviour is a complete waste of time and energy, but one that many people drift into without even realising. You may recognise these types of activities, such as surfing the Internet, gossiping face-to-face and over the phone or texting. Other activities include constant trips to the water cooler and frequent tea or coffee breaks often accompanied by chats with colleagues doing the same. A huge drain on your time is giving full and considered replies to unimportant emails that could be dealt with swiftly *after* you have completed priority tasks. The McKinsey Global Institute (Chui et al., 2012) conducted research into working practices and found that on average a full-time employee will spend up to two-and-a-half hours each day writing emails. They estimate that this adds up to an employee spending up to 81 days per year writing emails! Have you ever got to the end of the working day and thought that you had been busy only to find that you had achieved very little in terms of productive output? This is quite common and many workers report the same frustration. But if engaging in Mode 3 activities is so unproductive, why do so many people spend their precious time and energy on them? As I'll go on to explain in Chapter 5, left to its own devices the brain can behave like an unruly animal wandering off to seek more pleasurable activities after an initial period of focussed concentration on an important task. Mode 3 activities slip under your radar and offer many beguiling tasks that are easy, enjoyable and even give you a sense of achievement once you have completed them. One reason why people spend so much time on emails is that it gives them a sense of being busy without expending a great deal of mental effort. Another reason why people engage in Mode 3 activities is that they are recovering from the physical and mental demands of Mode 1 'firefighting' activities and they feel entitled to coast for a while. This usually leads to the boom-and-bust cycle I described earlier as these individuals put off doing important tasks until they become urgent emergencies.

Mode 4: nonurgent but productive activities

These are the types of activities that highly effective people spend most of their time on according to Stephen Covey (1999). If you think in terms of your investment of time and energy, this mode guarantees the highest yield in productivity. This is comparable to the oft-quoted Pareto principle (Koch, 2007) in the context of business, where 80 per cent of positive outcomes derive from 20 per cent of productive activities (e.g. 80 per cent of sales are made to 20 per cent of your client base). Mode 4 activities include:

Future planning

Investing time to develop medium- to long-term strategies for yourself, your team or organisation. All of the activities described in Chapter 3 fall into this category including taking stock of your values, setting career goals and breaking them down into achievable steps. This is an essential process for any organisation and is usually set down in a strategic plan with time scales. The essence of future planning is being proactive rather than reactive. Many people drift through life 'going with the flow', but if you don't have a sense of direction and purpose, the 'flow' can often carry you off to somewhere you'd rather not be.

Forging positive relationships

Unless your work can be done in isolation, developing and sustaining supportive relationships is an essential process. However, it often requires a significant investment of time to build trust and credibility, and you are unlikely to achieve any significant endeavour without support from other people. Paying attention to details such as following up on commitments you have made and acting in the spirit of reciprocity will help to nurture these relationships so that you can rely on them when the need arises.

Personal development

This could involve formal training or study, but could also include informal learning such as reading about your area of expertise. Many people adopt a passive approach to personal development and restrict themselves to mandatory training provided by their organisation. A proactive approach to personal development is to regard it as an investment in yourself so that you are not just more competent within your role, but also re-energised and enthusiastic about your work and constantly perfecting your 'craft'. Personal development should not just be restricted to work. Anything that contributes to your mental, physical and spiritual well-being and growth is vitally important but very often neglected. It's all too easy to put your feet up and watch TV after a hard day at work (a Mode 3 activity) but if you engage in a more meaningful activity, like maintaining your physical fitness or meditating, you will be rewarded with high energy and mental clarity the next day.

If you study the above activities closely you will see that although they're undoubtedly important, they don't have to be completed in the short or even medium term. That's why we often neglect activities that would make a huge difference to our professional and personal lives and expend much time and energy on less worthwhile tasks. If you don't have a sense of urgency driving you to act, it takes self-discipline and proactivity to prioritise Mode 4 activities and see them through until they are completed. You will always find something less taxing, more interesting or *seemingly* urgent to beguile you away from writing an important report or preparing for an exam. It's easy to fall into a *mañana* (wait until tomorrow) attitude if the task requires effort and can be put off. We naturally default to avoiding effort and seeking comfort because our ancient ancestor's survival relied on the conservation of energy and we have inherited this tendency. However, like many of our other primitive drives, sloth and conservation of energy may help with short-term survival, but work against any long-term ambitions we may have for improving our lives. The first step to evaluating how effectively you are investing your precious resources of time and energy is to carry out a detailed analysis of exactly how you are spending your time. In order to help you carry out this evaluation, I've provided a weekly activity log at Appendix 9.

Carrying out a time investment evaluation

At this point you may be thinking, 'Just what I need – another task!' And that's precisely the point. Although this is one more chore on top of your already busy schedule, it's a typical Mode 4 activity – not urgent but highly productive. If you put up with the short-term pain of completing the evaluation, you will be rewarded by saving precious time and increasing your productivity in the medium to long term. If you now feel sufficiently motivated, I'd like you to carry out the following steps:

1   Using the weekly activity log, record what you have been doing each hour over a five-day period.
2   Log each activity shortly after it has taken place so that you get an accurate recording of how you are spending your time. Avoid putting off the task until the end of the day or week so that you are able to capture the activities in detail.
3   Next, study each activity recorded and note which Mode it belongs to as M1, M2, M3 or M4.

Carrying out a detailed analysis of his activities enabled John to detect a number of less than optimum behavioural patterns that he hadn't been previously aware of (Table 4.6).

Table 4.6 John's weekly work activity log (Marketing Manager)

Day	Monday	Tuesday	Wednesday	Thursday	Friday
7–8am	Take the tube to work **M3**	Take the tube to work **M3**	Take the tube to work **M3**	Cycle to work **M4**	Cycle to work **M4**
8–9am	Coffee and a chat with Max **M3**	Prepare next week's client presentation **M4**	Prepare monthly performance report **M1**	Chamber of Commerce networking breakfast **M4**	Construct business case for new project **M1**
10–11am	Emails **M1**	Prepare next week's client presentation **M4**	Prepare monthly performance report **M1**	Organise team away day **M4**	Pitch business case to boss **M1**

Day	Monday	Tuesday	Wednesday	Thursday	Friday
11–12pm	Emails **M2**	2 phone calls (unscheduled) **M2**	Monthly line management meeting with boss **M1**	Book venue for team away day **M4**	Revise business case with boss' input **M4**
12–1pm	Telephone call from Jane in sales department **M2**	Telephone call Client complaint **M1**	Make revisions to monthly performance report & circulate **M1**	Conference call with boss **M1**	Circulate business case to team for comment **M4**
1–2pm	CPD lunch event **M4**	Drink with Matt from accounts **M3**	Lunchtime swimming class **M4**	Client networking lunch **M4**	Lunchtime meditation class **M4**
2–3pm	Chair departmental meeting **M1**	Visit Jane in sales department **M3**	Analyse departmental spending **M4**	Client site visit **M4**	Meet financial controller **M4**
3–4pm	Chair departmental meeting **M1**	Emails & coffee **M3**	Arrange meeting with financial controller **M4**	Client site visit **M4**	Prepare monthly finance report **M4**
4–5pm	Write up minutes of the meeting **M4**	Emails & coffee **M3**	Max dropped by for help (unscheduled) **M2**	Browsing in bookshop on way back to office **M3**	Prepare monthly finance report **M4**
5–6pm	Circulate minutes and plan weekly activities **M4**	Leave early Take tube home **M3**	Visit Jane in sales Convince her to come for drink with team **M3**	Coffee and a chat with Max **M3**	Plan weekly activities **M4**

John always knew that he had a tendency to 'ease himself into the week' on Mondays but hadn't fully acknowledged the amount of time he squanders on Mode 2 and 3 activities. He could cycle to work as part of his new fitness regime, but John takes the easy option followed by a chat over coffee with his friend Max. Having settled at his computer, John has to deal with a number of urgent emails for the first hour and his responses are necessary and productive. But then he drops down a gear and coasts for an hour, tinkering around with less productive emails that could be postponed or dealt with swiftly. Around midday, John receives a call from Jane who works in the sales department and is a bit of a flirt. John finds her attention very flattering and the conversation quickly turns from work matters to departmental gossip. Things get a bit more productive at lunchtime when John attends a continuous professional development (CPD) event and adds knowledge to his area of expertise. But time spent on Mode 2 and 3 activities in the morning means that John hasn't prepared sufficiently for chairing the departmental meeting in the afternoon and he finds the experience slightly stressful. Having learned his lesson, John decides to get ahead of the curve by spending time on Mode 4 tasks as he writes up and circulates the minutes from the meeting and carefully plans his activities for the rest of the week. John ends the day on a virtuous note by visiting the gym.

Studying the activity log for the rest of the week gave John further insights into his behaviour. He now realises that he has a tendency to 'reward' himself when he has engaged in a particularly productive task like preparing the client presentation a week ahead of schedule on Tuesday morning. Unfortunately this 'reward' resulted in a spot of lunchtime drinking with Matt and a lowering of inhibitions. The consequences of this episode were a gossipy visit to Jane followed by coffee and inconsequential emails for the rest of the afternoon. John can see that his productivity deserted him completely, leading to a lethargy spiral and an evening of slobbing around on the sofa watching TV. John also learns that a better way of recovering from Mode 1 urgent and productive activities, such as preparing the monthly performance report and meeting with his boss, is to invest time in Mode 4 rejuvenative activities like going swimming at lunchtime on Wednesday. He can see from the log that this type of activity re-energises him mentally and physically because he plunges himself into Mode 4 work tasks immediately after lunch, such as analysing departmental spending and meeting with the financial controller to pre-empt any problems with his budget arising. He notices a similar pattern emerging when he starts the day with a Mode 4 physical activity like cycling to work on Thursday and Friday. John notices that this really sets the tone for the day and provides him with the motivation and energy to engage with Mode 4 tasks or cope with the rigours of Mode 1 activities. He obtains a similar benefit from attending meditation classes at lunchtime – something that it's very hard to prioritise with a busy schedule as it involves slowing down and doing (apparently) very little. The results speak for themselves and John finishes the week on a productive high point.

The final lesson John learns from studying the activity log is that he often begins the week with sluggish, unproductive Mode 3 activities but gains increasing momentum throughout the week. It becomes apparent to John that if he consciously schedules Mode 4 activities on a Monday morning, he will obtain the energy boost needed to kick-start his week and gain momentum. Although this may seem a bit like jumping into a cold swimming pool first thing in the morning, studying the results convinces John that this short-term Mode 4 discomfort is much more rewarding in the medium term than slowly easing into the week with lazy, comfortable Mode 3 activities. And finally, John realises that if he cuts back on Mode 2 and 3 activities he will be able to spend more time on Mode 4 pre-emptive and highly productive work that prevents stressful Mode 1 emergencies from arising.

If you forget everything else I've taught you in this chapter, remember this:

1 Stress is an *external* event, something that happens to us in the workplace or elsewhere. The way we *think* about this event will largely determine how we *feel* and *act* in response to the stressor.
2 If you want to overcome worry and stress, increase your tolerance of uncertainty – inoculate yourself against anxiety!
3 Every time you engage in a challenge that takes you outside of your comfort zone, you make a deposit in your resilience capital.
4 Create a super-confident you by drawing on positive memories, role models or symbols of confidence.
5 Guard against other people stealing your time or lapsing into unproductive activities by default.
6 Try to spend as much time as possible on nonurgent but productive Mode 4 activities to increase productivity and avoid the need for firefighting.

References

Andrew, F.J., Gregory, J., Colflesh, H., and Wiley, W. (2012). Uncorking the muse: alcohol intoxication facilitates creative problem solving. *Consciousness and Cognition*, 21(1): 487–93.
Bunting, M. (2004). *Willing slaves: how the overwork culture is ruling our lives.* Harper Collins.
Chui, M. et al. (2012). *The social economy: unlocking value and productivity through social technologies.* McKinsey Global Institute.
Covey, S. (1999). *The 7 habits of highly effective people.* Simon Schuster.
Dugas, M.J. and Robichaud, R. (2007). *Cognitive-behavioural treatment for generalized anxiety disorder.* Routledge.
Gallagher, P. (2013). Slavery in the city. The Independent Newspaper.

Hackmann, A., Bennett-Levy, J. and Holmes, E.A. (2011). *Imagery in cognitive therapy*. Oxford University Press.

Health and Safety Executive (HSE). (2014). Stress-related and psychological disorders in Great Britain 2014.

Health and Safety Laboratory (HSL). (2003). Working long hours. Crown Copyright.

Kahneman, D. (2011). *Thinking, fast and slow*. Penguin Books.

Koch, R. (2007). *The 80/20 principle: The secret of achieving more with less*. Nicholas Brealey Publishing.

McCurry, J. (2015). Clocking off: Japan calls time on long hours culture. *Guardian Newspaper*.

Moore, C. (2014). *Margaret Thatcher, the authorised biography: not for turning, Volume one*. Penguin.

National Health Service (NHS). (2014). What is insomnia and how much sleep do we need? www.nhs.uk/conditions/insomnia/

Osborn, A.F. (2011). *Applied imagination: principles and procedures of creative writing*. Read Books.

Patmore, A. (2006). *The truth about stress*. Atlantic Books.

Price, G. (2013). *The promise: never have another negative thought again*. Pearson.

Shapiro, F. (2001). *Eye movement desensitization and reprocessing (EMDR)*. The Guilford Press.

Siegel, D. (2013). *Mindsight*. Oneworld Publications.

Tuckman, B.W. (1965). Developmental sequence in small groups. In *Psychological Bulletin* 1965, 63(4): 399, Naval Medical Research Institute, Bethesda, Maryland.

Chapter 5

Increasing your focus of attention

Have you ever experienced difficulty focussing your attention on a piece of work for a sustained period of time that you desperately needed to complete? Have you found yourself putting off tasks until the deadline approached and then completed them in a stressful frenzy of activity that left you feeling exhausted? It may be comforting to know that you're not alone and most people experience difficulty in managing their focus of attention at work or study. But if you *could* manage your focus of attention *at will*, think of what you could achieve and how this ability would give you a competitive edge in your chosen career.

One of our greatest challenges in the workplace is the need to maintain optimum levels of motivation and concentration, often in less than ideal conditions and when faced with a range of distractions. What differentiates individuals who are more likely to achieve success in life is their ability to manage impulses. Psychologist Walter Mischel carried out a famous experiment at Stanford University in the United States in the late 1960s, observing how four-year-old children manage to resist immediate gratification. The children were taken into a room and sat before a tempting marshmallow on a plate in front of them. The children were then told that they could eat the marshmallow at any time but if they waited for the adult to return after about 15 minutes, they would get an extra one as a reward. If you search on the Internet for 'Stanford Marshmallow Experiment', you will find a number of video clips of children struggling to resist temptation in order to get the reward. Many give in and eat the marshmallow before the adult returns, but the children who succeed manage their impulses by developing a number of strategies to distract themselves from temptation. This finding alone was quite a breakthrough at the time of the experiment. The next discovery that Mischel made was due to sheer serendipity.

By coincidence, Mischel's daughters attended Stanford University many years later along with a number of the children who had participated in the experiment. Mischel became interested in the stories his daughters told about these students as it became apparent that the children who had failed the marshmallow test were more likely to get into mishaps. His curiosity piqued, Mischel invested substantial academic resources in following up hundreds of adults who had participated in the experiment as children. The findings from this exercise were stunning: the individuals who had shown impulse control at the age of four were more likely to achieve higher levels of academic attainment, earn greater salaries and enjoy popularity. They were also less likely to gain excess weight or develop addiction to drugs. But why do we find it such a challenge to manage our impulses and stay focussed? Part of the reason seems to be the sheer amount of energy required to maintain these processes.

Psychologist Roy F. Baumeister notes that although our brain makes up 2 per cent of our body, it burns up 20 per cent of the body's energy (Baumeister and Tierney, 2011). His studies indicate that when we exercise willpower, we use up large amounts of glucose until we eventually become what he calls 'ego depleted', that is, less able to manage our thoughts, feelings and actions. Baumeister illustrates this tendency by drawing on a study carried out by Jonathan Levav and Shai Danziger (2011) in which they noted that judges in the Israeli prison system were more likely to deny parole (a less demanding decision) before a meal break than after it due to depleted glucose and willpower. The judges' exercise of mentally arduous tasks such as decision making is an example of what Nobel Prize winning psychologist Daniel Kahneman (2011) describes as System 2 thinking, any cognitive process that requires effort and concentration. If you're performing complex calculations, making important decisions or trying to empathise with someone during an important negotiation, you are likely to be engaging in System 2 thinking.

Kahenman makes the point that our cognitive default setting for most of the time is System 1 thinking, that is, making quick decisions with little or no reflection, being guided by impulses or learned reflexes. If you're driving a car through busy traffic and listening to the radio you are likely to be engaged in System 1 thinking. These mental shortcuts, or *heuristics*, conserve energy and help us to deal with the barrage of external stimuli that we are bombarded with throughout our daily lives. This type of quick thinking and acting has also helped us to survive over millions of years of evolution and is hard-wired into our brains. But this type of thinking can also be a lazy choice and lead us into distraction and poor decision making. The remainder of this chapter is aimed at helping you to develop your capacity for System 2 thinking.

Kime *and* mushin

One of the most important skills that you need to cultivate in order to maintain motivation and achieve your goals is the ability to focus your attention at will. At this point, I'd like to introduce you to the Japanese concepts of *kime* and *mushin* to illustrate the importance of developing total focus. In medieval Japan the Samurai were an elite warrior class who abided by a strict code of *bushido*: a code of conduct appropriate to warrior knights (Williams, 1975). The Samurai were expert in the art of swordsmanship and they also trained their minds to attain mental clarity and supreme focus even in the most dangerous of situations through the practice of Zen Buddhism. Zen master Takuan Soho stressed the importance of complete mental focus in combat by stressing that a moment's distraction from one's opponent can lead to defeat and, ultimately, death (1986, p. 20). According to this notion, if two Samurai are equally matched in terms of physical skill, the warrior who is able to maintain control of his mind is most likely to win the duel. This supreme focus of concentration is called *mushin* (literally translated as 'no-mindedness'), where the mind is completely calm and does not allow itself to be distracted by superfluous thoughts or the actions of the opponent. It's very similar to the experience of *flow* that we encountered in Chapter 3, where the individual is completely absorbed in each moment as it unfolds. This state of *mushin* facilitates the practice of *kime* (from the verb *kimeru*, 'to conclude'), or complete focus of mental and physical energy on the task in hand.

Although the Samurai had to deal with many challenging situations in feudal Japan, they didn't have to test their mental powers of focus in the modern workplace, where potential distractions are increasing exponentially due to multimedia and multitasking requirements. According to a recent study by the University of California (2009), American office workers are bombarded with 34 gigabytes of information each day, twice as much data as they were subjected to 30 years ago. UK and European working environments are probably quite similar. Common distractions include intrusions that Stephen Covey describes as 'urgent but not important' (1999), that is, they have the semblance of requiring urgent attention and are often linked to other people's priorities. You will recall from Chapter 4 that these intrusions include:

- Telephone calls
- Emails
- Text messages
- Dividing attention through multitasking
- Interruptions from coworkers

Studies have shown that it can take an average of 21 minutes to recover mental focus after one of these interruptions (Jackson, 2008) so they can have serious consequences for your work. However, these are *external* distractions; *internal* distractions are far more insidious. You may recall Mihal Csikszentmihalyi's description of psychological *entropy* that we encountered in Chapter 3, which describes how, without something to focus on, our minds have a tendency to ruminate about negative things that have happened in the past or worry about what might happen in the future. Our minds also have a tendency to drift away from the task in hand when it requires considerable mental effort (System 2 thinking). We are easily beguiled by more pleasurable cognitive experiences, very often without us being aware of it. This is what happened to Sarah.

Situation

Sarah works as a manager for a leading city recruitment consultancy and has to compile a quarterly summary of her team's overall performance against sales targets and circulate the report a week before the departmental meeting. She finds writing the report tedious and usually leaves it until the last moment, because only the mounting feeling of anxiety as the deadline looms can override her procrastination and distaste for the task. Sarah has only written one page of the report but feels incredibly bored already. The idea suddenly occurs to Sarah that she can make the report and the task far more interesting by benchmarking her team's performance against competitor organisations, and she takes the decision to do some online research.

Distraction

Sarah enters a series of words into the search engine with the aim of generating links to competitor organisations. She achieves her aim and is presented with a list of suitable options, but is also pleasantly surprised to see a link concerning her favourite TV series. Sarah responds instantly, without reflecting on her actions, and is directed to the TV series' official website, where she is delighted to find profiles of the different characters, free games and tunes.

Outcome

Sarah becomes absorbed in the character profiles and one item on the website seems to flow into the other. In fact, she's so engrossed in the website that it takes a colleague to remind Sarah that it's nearly lunchtime and she's shocked to find that she has just spent an hour and a half reading about her favourite TV series. With a growing sense of panic, Sarah realises that she has only written one page of a detailed report that is due for circulation by the end of the day. Consequently, she forgoes lunch in an attempt to make up for lost time and drinks several cups of coffee to boost her energy levels. However, skipping lunch causes Sarah's blood sugar to plummet and the combined effect of caffeine and anxiety at the looming deadline seriously impairs her concentration. She stays late and manages to circulate the report but is very unhappy about its overall quality and worries about its deficiencies being noticed by other colleagues, her manager in particular. Because Sarah has worked late, she misses her weekly workout at the gym and instead of returning home energised, she feels guilty, irritable and on edge. This level of physical arousal and her rumination and worry inevitably lead to a poor night's sleep.

You can see from this example that Sarah lost her focus of attention because the task in hand required a significant amount of System 2 thinking but she spontaneously defaulted to System 1 thinking at the prospect of a more pleasurable activity. This happened almost beyond her level of awareness. We will now explore a range of techniques to prevent you from falling into this trap and help you to cultivate a strong focus of attention.

1   Take control of your mind

Can you think of any occasions when your attention has drifted with negative consequences? Try to think of situations in which you are particularly vulnerable to this tendency. If you can foresee these traps, you will be more able to take positive action when you encounter them. It might be helpful to consider the fact that your mind often 'has a mind of its own' and is prone to wander off in different directions unless you take control of it. In psychological terms, the ability to take charge of

Table 5.1 Focus management log

Situation	Distraction	Outcome
What task was I engaged in?	At what point did I become distracted? How did this happen?	What were the consequences of becoming distracted?

your thinking processes is called *executive function* (Wells, 2009) and you can strengthen this ability in the same way that you can build muscles by working out with weights in a gym. Every time you notice your mind wandering and gently bring it back to focus on the task in hand is the equivalent to carrying out a repetition with a dumbbell to strengthen your bicep muscle. Use Table 5.1 and Appendix 10 to monitor your mind's tendency to wander for one whole day and note down the situation, type of distraction and outcome. This is the first step to strengthening your *executive function*.

2   Clear your mind

Every day presents us with a range of conflicting priorities that continually distract us and weaken our focus of attention. We often get caught up in what Stephen Covey describes as 'the thick of thin things' (Covey, 1999), including other people's priorities and insubstantial activities that make us feel busy but seldom lead to significant achievements. Clear your mind of any nagging responsibilities by writing a daily task list ranked in order of priority. Once you have an overview of the tasks that need to be achieved during the work day you can focus on their completion sequentially and will be far less prone to the capricious state of *monkey mind* that we encountered in Chapter 3. Try to cultivate the Samurai practice of *mushin*, clearing your mind of all extraneous thoughts before you commence a task.

3   Optimise your working environment

If your working environment is cluttered, you will be at a distinct psychological disadvantage before you've even engaged with the first task. This is because your focus of attention will be distracted by uncomfortable visible reminders of other unfinished tasks (Allen, 2002) and nothing weighs more heavily on our sense of motivation than an overflowing inbox. Once you have decluttered your working area, try to anticipate what you will need in order to complete your tasks and have them to hand. If you have to wander off to borrow a calculator, for example, you are far more likely to lose your focus of concentration and get drawn into a conversation (often willingly to distract yourself from the mental rigours of the task). It will also help you to maintain focus if you can close down all other media that are likely to cause interruptions until you have completed your task. If it takes you 21 minutes to recover your mental focus (Jackson, 2008), ask yourself if you need really to receive emails and phone calls while you are trying to complete a piece of work. It may be much better to return calls and attend to emails once you have completed your mission.

4   Focus on the task in hand

The Buddhist practice of *one-pointedness*, or *ekaggata* (Gorkom, 1993), provides an antidote to the fragmented concentration that we constantly experience as a result of the pressure to multitask in the modern workplace. The practice of making each action the complete focus of your attention can lead to a state of consciousness described as the 'unification of the mind', similar to the experience of *flow* described in Chapter 3. You could regard each working day as an opportunity to develop this state of consciousness, but it requires *intent* on your behalf. When you commence a particular task, you need to commit yourself to its completion with total focus of concentration and without interruption as much as is practically possible. This may require breaking down larger tasks into more manageable units (e.g. lasting an hour at a time) as it will be difficult to sustain this intense level of concentration for extended periods.

5   Don't allow your mind to wander

If you have spent a day using the Focus Management Log, you should be able to notice the way in which your mind pulls away from the task in hand and anticipate when you are most vulnerable to distraction. Sometimes the mind can act like a lazy animal, constantly avoiding effort, taking shortcuts (type 1 thinking) and seeking pleasurable experiences. It needs constant, gentle encouragement to focus on work that might require effort in the short term (type 2 thinking) but will lead to a reward in the medium to long term. Your challenge is to arrest the mind's impulse to wander off and coax it back to work. A strategy that can help you to achieve this level of control is to regard any intruding thoughts or impulses as *buses* or *trains*: you can simply watch them go by without being carried away by them. Also, it's pointless trying to battle with these thoughts and impulses by trying to block them out, in the same way that it would be unhelpful to stand in the middle of the road and stop the traffic. Taking a detached view of your random thoughts and impulses and gently bringing your focus back to the task in hand is a far more effective strategy.

6   Nourish your mind

Two thirds of your brain consists of fatty acids so that if you eat a diet rich in omega-3 you are literally feeding your brain thus improving cognitive functioning and emotional stability (Servan-Schreiber, 2003). You can obtain omega-3 supplements from any chemist or health food store. Alternatively, foods that are rich in omega-3 include tuna, mackerel, herring, sardines, salmons and eggs. Vegetarian options include walnuts, spinach, seaweed and watercress. Whilst at work, light snacks that are low in carbohydrates are excellent for maintaining optimum levels of mental energy. These include fruit, green vegetables, salads, nuts, meat and fish and come under the umbrella of low glycemic index (GI) food. White bread, pasta and potatoes fall under the category of high GI food because your body converts these nutrients into glucose much faster than low GI food (Baumeister and Tierney, 2011). Eating a cake or other high GI snack will give you an instant blast of mental vitality but will inevitably lead to a drop in energy as your glucose level plummets soon after, leading to further cravings for sugary or starchy snacks. Low GI foods help you to avoid this boom and bust cycle by providing a steady supply of glucose to the brain. It's also tempting to rely on caffeinated drinks to sharpen concentration, but excessive consumption leads to a similar negative cycle of brief bursts of mental energy followed by descent into lethargy and the craving for another 'fix'. Caffeinated drinks are also diuretic, so your work will be interrupted by constant trips to the toilet. Try to get into the habit of sipping water throughout the day. Your brain is 80 per cent water, so you need to keep it consistently hydrated to maintain high levels of concentration.

7   Pace yourself

You need to take regular breaks to maintain focus, but be careful to avoid displacement activities (surfing the Internet for example) that deplete your concentration and energy levels. Try to toil persistently on a specific task for a set period of time and then take a short break away from your work area if possible. If your job is sedentary, make sure you move around during breaks to relieve muscular tension and sore eyes from staring at a computer screen. Any activity that moderately raises your heart rate and respiratory level will increase the amount of oxygen to your brain and improve overall concentration. A brisk walk at lunchtime is an excellent way of reinvigorating your mind and body and will repay the time you invest with better productivity when you return to work.

8   Stretch yourself

One of the major challenges that we experience when confronted with work tasks is the way we view them. If you tell yourself that the assignment you are faced with will be mental torture, this will become a self-fulfilling prophecy. Even the most fortunate individuals have to complete tasks they find demanding or boring and most successful people have developed mental resilience to overcome these challenges. Instead of contemplating the prospect of sustained mental effort as an unpleasant chore, try to reframe it as an opportunity to develop *mental stamina and optimum focus*. Your career success will depend on your ability to cultivate these two virtues and deploy them at will in the same way that top athletes need to develop excellent physical stamina.

9   Give yourself a reward

You can improve your level of motivation by regularly rewarding yourself for the completion of tasks. The size of the reward can be calibrated against the scale of the achievement. For example, you could reward yourself with a sip of water after writing a paragraph with total focus or walk to the water cooler and stretch your legs after spending an hour completing a whole section of a report. In psychological terms, you will be strengthening focus through *positive reinforcement* so that your brain begins to associate sustained concentration and mental effort with a pleasant reward.

If you forget everything else I've taught you in this chapter, remember this:

1   Increasing impulse control leads to a better chance of success in life.
2   We are constantly bombarded by distractions in the workplace and it can take up to 21 minutes to recover our focus of attention.
3   De-clutter your work area and focus on one task at a time.
4   Every time you notice your mind wandering and bring it back to focus, you develop 'mental muscle' and strengthened *executive function*.
5   Exercising our willpower uses up huge amounts of physical energy. We need to choose our focus of attention carefully.
6   Your mind is a highly complex physical organ. It needs excellent nutrition and hydration to function optimally.

References

Allen, D. (2002). *Getting things done*. Piatkus.

Baumeister, R.F. and Tierney, J. (2011). *'Willpower': rediscovering our greatest strength*. Allen Lane.

Covey, S. (1999). *The 7 habits of highly effective people*. Simon Schuster.

Danziger, S., Levav, J. and Avnaim-Pesso, L. (2011). Breakfast, lunch and their effect on judicial decisions. Proceedings of the National Academy of Sciences.

Gorkom, N.V. (1993). *The world in the buddhist sense*. Triple Gem Press.

Jackson, M. (2008). *Distracted: the erosion of attention and the coming dark age*. Prometheus Books.

Kahneman, D. (2011). *Thinking, fast and slow*. Penguin Books.

Servan-Schreiber, D. (2003). *Healing without Freud or Prozac*. Rodale.

Soho, T. (1986). *The unfettered mind: writings from a Zen Master to a sword master*. Translated by William Scott Wilson. Kodansha International Ltd.

Wells, A. (2009). *Metacognitive therapy for anxiety and depression*. Guilford Press.

Williams, B. (1975). *Know karate-do*. William Luscombe Publisher.

Chapter 6

Using interpersonal skills for maximum effect

Your ability to create and nurture professional relationships with colleagues and clients is one of the most important skills you need to develop because it will almost certainly make the difference between success or failure in your chosen career. Daniel Goleman (1996) famously defined the concept of *emotional intelligence* (EI) and maintains that possessing this quality is a greater predictor of success than intelligence quotient (IQ), which is measured using a range of standardised tests. You may have come across individuals who have very high levels of technical skill and knowledge but who are weak in terms of their interpersonal skills. They might have poor emotional regulation and frequently reveal their anger and irritation, alienating people around them. They may also possess low levels of empathy and are unable to see things from the perspective of the other person they are interacting with and fail to create a positive rapport. Conversely, you can probably think of individuals who are commonly described a 'team players' who may not possess in-depth technical skills but are charismatic and able to use their interpersonal skills to motivate people with perhaps greater knowledge to work together towards a shared endeavour.

Although Goleman's claims about emotional intelligence have been contested by some academics, the concept of EI has had a major impact on the world of employment and education and the subject is even being taught in UK state secondary schools (Hastings, 2004). Organisations throughout the world place an increased emphasis on recruiting candidates for all roles who are able to demonstrate excellent emotional intelligence as well as technical skills. I want to introduce you to a range of methods that will help you to develop excellent rapport with colleagues and clients in the workplace but also assert yourself if you have to. Unfortunately, assertiveness has become an essential skill in an increasingly competitive professional arena, so it's better to know you have a range of strategies to fall back on if a challenging situation arises. To start with, I want to explore with you a very subtle area that will help you to manage your psychological reactions during interpersonal interactions within the workplace and their effect on your mood and behaviour, particularly when you are confronted with stressful or competitive situations. Let's look at the following example.

Frank's challenge

Frank has just undergone a highly competitive recruitment and selection process and has been appointed to the role of sales account manager with an organisation called Saber Communications. His initial feelings of euphoria at winning the role are beginning to subside as he contemplates attending a five-day residential training course as part of his induction to the organisation. Frank is aware of a growing sense of unease that he finds hard to admit to anyone, including his wife. He won't know anyone on the course and he is aware of the highly competitive organisational culture. He knows that the induction courses are designed to test character and even, he suspects, weed out unsuitable candidates post-recruitment. Given this type of environment, Frank anticipates that all of the other candidates will make every effort to impress the course supervisors. Frank's main concern is that he won't be able to shine in this pressurised situation and he worries about making a negative impression that will stay with him throughout his career with the company if, indeed, he survives the induction course.

Many work situations require skilful social interaction, including conferences, induction courses and team building days. If you find yourself faced with an unfamiliar social situation like Frank, it's perfectly understandable for you to feel some concern, particularly if the outcome may affect your career. However, it's vitally important for you to develop an awareness of any unhelpful thoughts and actions that you may engage in when you find yourself in pressurised social interactions as they may compromise your ability to manage the situation optimally. Even more importantly, you need to develop an effective range of responses to turn these situations to your advantage.

Professor David Clark and Dr Adrian Wells (1995) have developed a model of social phobia that has been proved effective through many clinical trials and is widely used within CBT as part of a method for helping people overcome social anxiety. Although you may consider yourself to be a generally confident and outgoing person who is not in any way socially phobic, using aspects of Clark and Wells' model will help you to reduce nervousness and boost confidence in social interactions and also help you to identify areas for improving your interpersonal skills. First, I want to introduce you to some of the characteristics of social anxiety and ask you to consider whether you have experienced one or more of these at any point in your life. My hunch is that most of us experience some social anxiety at some stage and this will vary in intensity depending on the circumstances, the individual and their personal history. The point is, if we gain insight into why we become anxious and develop strategies for gaining confidence, we can excel in social interactions.

The psychology of social interaction

Many people suffer from social anxiety. Symptoms are on a spectrum from mild self-consciousness that can be addressed through social skills training, right through to paralysing social phobia that requires a clinical intervention. The *Diagnostic and Statistical Manual of Mental Disorders* (*DSM-5*) is *the* bible for psychiatrists, psychologists and other mental health workers and the latest manual (2013) records the prevalence of social anxiety as approximately 7 per cent within the United States population. Episodes of social anxiety are frequently experienced in the workplace because individuals are more likely to feel that they are being scrutinised by other people and evaluated in some way. These individuals fear that they may be judged negatively by other colleagues or supervisors for failing to perform certain tasks in some way. Common examples include public speaking, communicating with others individually or in small groups and writing or eating in public. Social anxiety is triggered by the belief that the person concerned will act in a way that others will disapprove of and that they will be rejected by the other person or the group (this is very similar to the cognitive and behavioural consequences for *shame* that we encountered in the emotions table in Chapter 1).

Why do we as human beings often suffer from this fear of being rejected by others so acutely? A number of evolutionary psychologists including Leary (2001) have developed the theory that this fear of rejection from the group helped our ancient ancestors to survive and has been passed down to us through natural selection. Imagine that you are part of a hunter-gatherer clan or a small agricultural community clinging to life in the midst of an inhospitable terrain. Resources are scarce and survival depends on the group obtaining sufficient food, shelter and warmth from the camp fire. The world outside of the group is a terrifying wilderness where wild animals and human predators stalk their prey, particularly at night. The prospect of being cast out of the group would almost certainly mean a lonely death and we can imagine our ancient ancestors being hypervigilant for any signs that they had fallen out of favour within the clan.

This fear of being ostracised persists throughout centuries and examples can be found in literature as diverse as the Bible and the tales of the brothers Grimm (2014), in which unfortunate characters like Hansel and Gretel are banished to the forbidding darkness of the forest. Modern day examples include William Golding's *Lord of the Flies* (1954) in which a group of boys stranded on an island descend into primitive tribal savagery or even Stephen King's *Carrie* (1974), in which a shy adolescent girl is rejected by her high school peers with horrific consequences. Fear of being ostracized now has a modern manifestation in being 'unfriended' on social media and examples of cyber bullying are widely reported within the media. It's little wonder that we may feel slightly apprehensive when joining a new work 'clan' for the first time and if economic circumstances mean that resources are scarce, the prospect of being cast out into corporate wilderness can weigh on our minds. Let's have a look at the way in which social anxiety gets triggered and what we can do to reverse the process.

As mentioned in Chapter 1, when we engage in unhelpful anxious thinking, this process usually triggers a negative emotional response that we experience *physically*. Hartmann (1983, pp. 435–456) emphasises the fact that when the social anxiety process gets triggered, we are likely to focus on these physical symptoms in addition to concern about our performance and what others think of us. As we become increasingly self-conscious and pay attention to these physical sensations and thoughts (internal), our focus gets hijacked from what's going on in the social situation (external), making interaction with the other person or group even more challenging. This can then lead to us making negative *inferences* about what the other person is thinking, jumping to subjective conclusions that they may be making negative judgements about us or what we have to say. Look at what happens to Frank when he attends the residential training course.

As you can see in Figure 6.1, Frank is worried about the possibility that he will appear nervous and that other people will perceive this as a sign of weakness, so he engages in a number of *safety behaviours*. When people become socially anxious they typically engage in these types of behaviours, including avoiding eye contact or rehearsing what they are going to say to make sure they sound articulate and intelligent. Other examples include playing with their mobile phone, making excuses and leaving the social situation or drinking alcohol to gain confidence.

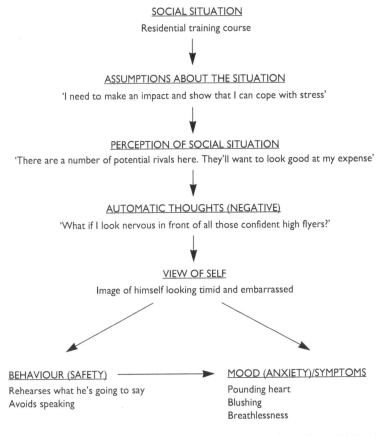

SOCIAL SITUATION
Residential training course

ASSUMPTIONS ABOUT THE SITUATION
'I need to make an impact and show that I can cope with stress'

PERCEPTION OF SOCIAL SITUATION
'There are a number of potential rivals here. They'll want to look good at my expense'

AUTOMATIC THOUGHTS (NEGATIVE)
'What if I look nervous in front of all those confident high flyers?'

VIEW OF SELF
Image of himself looking timid and embarrassed

BEHAVIOUR (SAFETY)
Rehearses what he's going to say
Avoids speaking

MOOD (ANXIETY)/SYMPTOMS
Pounding heart
Blushing
Breathlessness

Figure 6.1 Behavioural analysis model for Frank. Adapted from Clark, D.M. and Wells, A. (1995). A cognitive model of social phobia. In R. Heimberg, M. Liebowitz, D.A. Hope and F. R. Schneier (Eds), *Social phobia: diagnosis, assessment and treatment.* Copyright Guilford Press. Reprinted with permission of The Guilford Press.

The problem with these safety behaviours is that they bring about the very thing that the person fears will happen. For example, if Frank avoids eye contact and doesn't say very much, the person that he is interacting with may think that he is aloof or does not like them and may make their excuses to conclude the conversation and move on. In this instance, Frank's fear of rejection becomes a self-fulfilling prophecy and increases his anxiety in subsequent social interactions.

You can use the Clark and Wells model to analyse your behaviour during social interactions at work, particularly when there are stressful aspects associated with the event. Typical examples include meetings, performance appraisals, attending conferences or training days, team building events or even social events like the office Christmas party. Try to spot recurrent patterns of behaviour that would benefit from improvement by analysing recent events. When you're next faced with a situation at work that requires skilful social interaction, it's worth bearing in mind the following points.

Consider what assumptions you are making about the situation

In Chapter 1 we explored the way in which people may develop unhelpful negative beliefs in childhood that remain dormant until they are triggered by a specific event. The workplace, with its many social interactions that we engage in on a daily basis, can project us back to vulnerable childlike states of being. Take Frank. Although he has managed to build a successful career and project an air of confidence most of the time, he has memories of always being the last person in his class to be chosen for team events on school sports days. As a child he formed the belief that he wasn't popular and that other people were better than him in some way. Although he feels fine about himself most of the time, Frank's unhelpful belief gets triggered whenever he enters social situations, particularly those in which he doesn't know anyone and there is an element of competition. If you notice a pattern of feeling vulnerable in social situations, it may be worth asking yourself where these feelings are coming from. Is this your 'younger self' feeling vulnerable? You can then remind yourself that you are a capable adult and don't have to feel threatened in this situation. It's also worth considering whether you are engaging in *all or nothing thinking* about the situation and making unrealistic demands upon yourself. If you tell yourself that you *have* to appear informed, witty and intelligent in front of others, you will undoubtedly increase the amount of stress you experience as part of the social interaction. Try instead to develop the intention of creating a positive impression, but don't feel you have to try too hard.

* Do you see any threats in the social situation?
  If you find yourself feeling apprehensive at the prospect of engaging in a social situation, try not to raise the stakes too high in your mind by telling yourself how *awful* the interaction will be if you

aren't sufficiently witty, charming and charismatic. Most social interactions are pretty average and even if they fall flat, you can still learn from them.

• How do you view yourself in social situations?
  It's perfectly normal to feel some nervousness in social situations, particularly if you are meeting other people for the first time at a conference, training course or new job, for example. The big mistake a lot of people make, and one that you need to avoid, is just because you *feel* slightly nervous it does not mean that you will *appear* nervous to others. It's quite an easy mistake to make because the physical experience of even moderate levels of anxiety is so acute that we automatically believe the symptoms are visibly apparent to others. Perhaps you can recall an occasion when your face became slightly flushed or you could detect a few beads of perspiration forming on your brow. This is hardly noticeable to others but if you think you're being closely scrutinised, it feels like an illuminated sign on your head.

Many people who suffer from social anxiety develop unhelpful mental images of themselves the way they think others see them – in Frank's case he had an image of himself looking timid, flushed and embarrassed and was convinced that was what other person could see. This leads to another mistake: checking whether the other person has noticed any initial social awkwardness that you may be feeling by closely studying their facial expressions and body language. The problem with this approach is that you are trying to analyse ambiguous information and if you are experiencing any anxiety at all, you'll be more prone to making errors of judgement. I once gave a presentation to over a hundred managers and felt very nervous. After I had started speaking, I noticed a woman in the second row staring at me with a grim expression and concluded that, (a) she was intensely annoyed by what I was saying and (b) my flies were undone. These *inferences* increased my anxiety level and nearly ruined the presentation. During the break I felt compelled to find out what the woman had found so objectionable in my presentation and I approached her with that question. She appeared completely baffled when I told her that she had looked offended and then said, 'Oh, that's my thinking face.' The point is that it's rarely the case that others will notice your anxiety or social awkwardness, but if you search hard enough for a reaction, you'll find the evidence and your concern will become a self-fulfilling prophecy.

The final point I want to make is that I have successfully treated many people for social anxiety and an important part of the procedure involves getting them to rate how nervous they appear to others and in what way (e.g. blushing, sweating, shaking, etc.). I then film them engaged in social interaction with another person (after much protesting) and get them to predict how nervous they will appear when the video recording is played back to them. In virtually every case they are stunned to see how unnoticeable their physical symptoms of anxiety are. This procedure alone makes a dramatic impact in reducing social anxiety, which is why Professor Clark introduced it as an important part of the protocol. Bear that in mind next time you think other people will notice any nervousness that you may be feeling.

Ignore your butterflies

As I mentioned previously, when we find social situations stressful, we are highly likely to focus on physical and cognitive symptoms of anxiety. This leads us to fixate on our increased heartbeat and racing mind, interpreting these symptoms as signs that the situation is going badly and leading to a vicious cycle of further anxiety and associated physiological arousal. It's important for you to realise that these initial feelings of nervousness or 'butterflies' at the beginning of the social interaction are temporary and will fly away if you ignore them; but if you remain focussed on your butterflies, you'll stir them up even more. The best strategy you can adopt under these circumstances is to move your focus of attention away from the internal (physical sensations of nervousness) to the external (where you are and the person you're talking to). I'll elaborate on this strategy in the next section.

Banish safety behaviours

Many people use alcohol as a social lubricant and a couple of drinks at a party to get you in the mood is OK; but using booze to gain confidence could have disastrous consequences in a work setting. There are far too many examples of unfortunate individuals becoming disinhibited through excessive drinking at office parties only to wake up to a bad hangover and a wrecked career. Another tendency to watch out for is making excuses, like going to the toilet or the bar, to end the conversation if you start to feel awkward. You may feel a temporary sense of relief when you escape the situation, but if you do this too often you'll strengthen the belief that you can't cope when similar situations arise. One of the most common safety behaviours that people engage when they feel awkward in social situations is *mentally rehearsing* what to say before they verbalise their next sentence. The main reason for this behaviour is that many of us put pressure on ourselves by believing that we *have to* appear witty and articulate at all times, so we try to formulate the best sentence we can come up with. A related safety behaviour is *monitoring* our delivery while we are actually speaking to check whether we sound sufficiently intelligent, profound and so on. Both of these behaviours create problems within the social interaction.

First, if you get caught up in rehearsing what you are going to say, the conversation may have moved on by the time you have constructed your scintillating contribution and you risk losing the thread completely. Second, excessively monitoring your delivery will make you feel self-conscious and inhibit the creative flow of your thinking during the conversation. The third trap that people fall into is carrying out a mental 'post-mortem' of the sentence they have just delivered, evaluating their performance and its impact and also checking for any errors. This again leads to heightened self-consciousness and the risk of losing the thread of the conversation. The most effective strategy that you can use in social interactions to cut through anxiety and increase confidence is the practice of *focussed attention* and *active listening*. You can start by tuning into the external environment paying particular attention to what you can see and hear. Next, really focus on the person you are engaging with and the content of the conversation. Try to get into the flow of the conversation moment-by-moment as though you are having a verbal dance with the other person, giving, taking and being spontaneous in your responses. As you get caught up in the momentum of the conversation without overthinking your contribution, any initial nervousness will dissolve, and as you begin to relax, different insights will occur to you spontaneously.

Finally, if you've become aware of any safety behaviours that you've been engaging in, set yourself the task of banishing them one by one. Push yourself outside of your comfort zone when engaging in social interactions. Instead of constantly playing the role of a 'good listener', increase your contribution each time (obviously don't try to dominate the conversation) and then objectively analyse how the interaction went. It will help you to develop confidence by setting up social interactions at work as 'experiments' in which you make a prediction in terms of how you think you will perform and then objectively measure the outcome. Here's an example of one of Frank's experiments after he survived the induction course.

Situation: Monthly performance review with my line manager.

Prediction: I reckon that I'll become self-conscious and nervous when talking to my manager and I'm 100 per cent certain that he'll notice it.

Experiment: The way I'm going to test my prediction is, first of all, by dropping all of the safety behaviours that I use in these situations. These include always taking a cup of coffee with me rather than a glass of water in case I need to 'rev my brain up'. I also overcompensate for my nerves by trying very hard to look and sound dynamic and energetic instead of being natural and quietly confident. I also pay particular attention to any physical sensations of nervousness like my heart racing or my face feeling slightly flushed. This time I'm going to ignore these feelings as much as possible and focus my attention on presenting the performance report. The next thing I'm going to do is be as objective as possible in assessing my boss's response to me after I've dropped my safety behaviours. The only way I can know for certain that he's noticed my nervousness is if he says something about it. If I just go by his facial expression or tone of voice, my nerves could make me jump to the wrong conclusion.

Outcome: The meeting went better than I expected. I felt nervous to start with, particularly as I didn't have my cup of coffee to fall back on. As I became focussed on the task of presenting the performance data and communicating with my boss, I became more relaxed. The initial nervousness made me mentally sharper and, because I dispensed with the coffee, I didn't go into my usual slightly manic overdrive. My boss complimented me on my team's performance and didn't make any mention of me appearing nervous.

What did I learn? I learned that if I prepare for the meeting adequately, I don't have to put on an act of appearing super-dynamic because that will just increase my nervousness and self-consciousness. I realise that the coffee's not helpful at all as it makes me feel even more jittery and muddle-headed, so I'm better off with water. My slight pre-meeting nervousness gives me a shot of adrenaline and that's enough to sharpen up my mental faculties while I'm presenting. Finally, I've learned that if I focus on communicating with my boss during the meeting rather than on how I'm feeling, my nervousness declines. I still feel 20 per cent certain that I'll become nervous and that my boss will notice at the next meeting because I may have been lucky this time. I know that I need to keep pushing myself by dropping my safety behaviours if I want to increase my confidence in these situations.

Now it's your turn. Use the worksheet at Appendix 7 along with these guidelines:

Prediction: Choose a situation that will take you outside of your comfort zone and help you to develop more confidence in managing social interactions within the workplace.

- What do you worry will happen in the situation? Be as specific as possible.
- On a scale of 0 to 100 per cent, how likely is this to occur?
- How can you objectively judge that what you predicted has occurred? Remember, body language and facial expressions can be ambiguous indicators, particularly when you are nervous.

Experiment: How can you test your predictions in the situation? One of the best methods for doing this is to drop your safety behaviours and see what happens, but try to remain objective at all times and don't fall into the trap of *emotional reasoning* (e.g. evaluating the situation based exclusively on how you felt at the time).

Outcome: Evaluate the situation whilst being as analytical and dispassionate as possible. What *actually* happened? Exactly how accurate was your prediction?

What did you learn from the experiment? Having gone outside of your comfort zone and dropped your safety behaviours, what important lessons have you learned about yourself? If you had to rate the likelihood of your prediction occurring in a similar situation on a scale of 0 to 100 per cent, what would it be? Very importantly, what would you need to do in order to get that rating down to 0 per cent?

Asserting yourself in the workplace

Being able to think and act assertively in the workplace is a skill you can learn – it isn't an innate quality you are born with. Even if you work in the least competitive of environments, the need to assert yourself will undoubtedly arise on occasion. In spite of this, many people fail to assert themselves because they have formed unhelpful beliefs about this type of behaviour, for example, that they *shouldn't* act in a confrontational way. However, if you continually fail to assert yourself when conflicts of opinion arise in the workplace (and life in general), you run the risk of gradually eroding your self-confidence by re-enforcing the belief that you haven't got the resources to deal with these situations. Consider whether any of the following apply to you:

1   Do you have a tendency to 'go with the flow' and let other colleagues get their own way, sometimes at your own expense?

2   Do you frequently refrain from expressing your opinions if you suspect others will disagree with you?

3   Do you believe that disagreement with others may lead to you becoming less popular?

4   During meetings or discussions with colleagues, do you often find yourself holding back expressing what you consider to be a good idea until you sense the general opinion of the group?

5   Do you avoid confrontations at all costs for fear of 'making waves' and because you don't think that you could cope with the consequences?

6   If someone offends you in some way, do you avoid bringing the matter to the other person's attention but feel resentful after the event?

7   If you find yourself struggling with a particular task, do you experience difficulty in asking others for support or guidance because you believe that they will think less of you?

8   Do you feel awkward negotiating benefits for yourself within the workplace, such as pay rises, annual leave or the possibility of promotion, because you find the prospect of refusal anxiety provoking?

9   Have you ever found yourself letting resentment build up over a period of time and thinking, 'I'm not going to take this anymore', followed by an angry outburst towards others?

10 Do you feel compelled to win every argument and get your own way all of the time for fear of letting others get one up on you and appearing a loser?

11 Do you frequently criticise and blame others when you become frustrated with their performance?

12 Have you occasionally used harsh verbal communication, swearing or raising your voice in an attempt to dominate others?

13 Do you try to intimidate others by using aggressive body language, gestures and eye contact?

14 Do you feel silently resentful towards others for taking advantage of you and fantasise about getting your own back?

15 Have you got your own back on someone by criticising them to other colleagues in the hope that it will damage their reputation?

16 Have you ever agreed to take on a task but felt silently resentful and then deliberately failed to complete it on time or turned out poor quality work?

17 Have you ever let work pressures build up without drawing atten-
    tion to the situation and then taken sick leave to make the point that
    you are overburdened and put upon?
18 Do you communicate your disapproval by remaining resentfully
    silent and displaying negative body language?

If you found yourself answering mostly 'yes' to questions 1–8, this indicates that you may have an overtly *passive* style of behaviour and communication. Responses to questions 9–13 indicate an *aggressive* style,
whilst responses to questions 14–18 denote *passive-aggressive* behaviour. Let's consider each of these behavioural styles in turn and look
at the disadvantages associated with them. This will also help you to
recognise these behaviour patterns in others and develop strategies for
dealing with them.

Passive behaviour

At its most fundamental level, passive behaviour is an attempt to avoid
emotional discomfort (predominantly anxiety or guilt) that arises when
the individual contemplates asserting themselves. This is because they
maintain the belief that other people's opinions, needs and desires are
more important than their own. The psychologist Jeffery E. Young
describes this as the *subjugation life trap* (Young and Klosko, 1994).
These individuals consistently place other peoples' needs ahead of their
own and they may let others control them either in the workplace or in
personal relationships. They fear hurting other people's feelings by putting their needs first or are afraid they will be rejected or punished in
some way if they assert themselves. Their childhoods are often characterised by controlling or punishing parents; they learned as children to
subjugate their needs for fear of abandonment. Typically they enter into a
vicious cycle of avoiding emotional discomfort at the prospect of asserting themselves, feeling temporary relief but failing to learn that they can
tolerate strong emotions and deal with the situation.

The downside of passive behaviour: The problem with this type of
behaviour is that it allows individuals with the tendency to bully and take
advantage of others to repeatedly walk all over passive people knowing
full well that they won't object. This often happens in work environments
as well as personal relationships. The passive person's attempts to avoid
emotional discomfort by failing to assert themselves continually feeds
and strengthens their unhelpful belief that they are less worthy than others and incapable of standing up for their rights (Figure 6.2). In the long

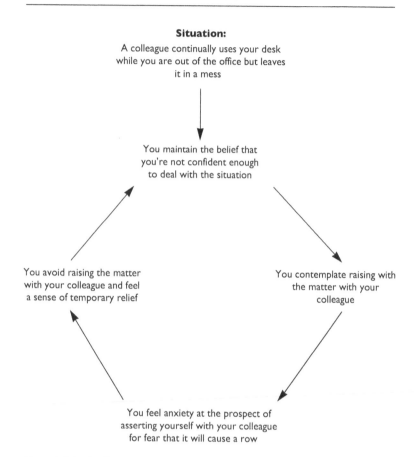

Figure 6.2 Lack of assertiveness cycle.

term this low self-esteem, sense of helplessness and resentment of others can lead to depression. Also, failure to be clear about one's needs confuses other people so that they misinterpret the passive person's words or actions, perpetuating the situation that is causing them discomfort.

What to do when confronted with passive behaviour: If you recognise passive behaviour in colleagues you are working with or managing, some of the following approaches may prove useful:

• Bear in mind that this person may suffer from low self-esteem in spite of their outward appearance of making jokes and appearing self-deprecating. Consider your choice of words carefully so that you don't run the risk of being seen as punishing or critical.

- If you are in a group or one-to-one situation with the person, try to draw them in by using nonthreatening open questions and express a genuine interest in their opinion on the matter in hand.
- If you don't think you're getting their true opinion on an issue, you might ask them to play 'devil's advocate' for your benefit and come up with as many potential flaws in the proposal as possible to increase its robustness.
- If you are working collaboratively, try to encourage the passive person to make decisions and agree on responsibilities with you jointly. Don't let them get away with deferring to you on all matters.

Passive-aggressive behaviour

In its most extreme manifestation, this type of behaviour is diagnosed as passive-aggressive personality disorder (American Psychiatric Association, 2013). However, in the majority of cases, these individuals find it difficult to assert themselves on the one hand, but feel deeply resentful about not getting their needs met and express this resentment indirectly. This can take the form of sulking, criticising other colleagues behind their backs, appearing withdrawn, consistently being late for meetings, deliberately failing to meet deadlines or live up to the responsibilities of one's job or playing the role of 'victim' to shame others or gain sympathy. Psychological theories suggest that this behaviour is formed in early childhood in circumstances where parents are overly controlling (Murphy & Hoff Oberlin, 2005). In these circumstances the child may avoid expressing their needs and feelings for fear of disapproval or even punishment. This suppression of the child's needs eventually leads to resentment towards the parents and passive acts of rebellion, repeated in later life with authority figures. Often children with controlling or punishing parents develop low self-esteem in adulthood and any perceived slight will lead to feelings of anger. Unfortunately, they are unable to communicate their anger in an open, constructive way, so they express it covertly through passive-aggressive actions or communication.

The downside of passive-aggressive behaviour: The big problem with this type of behaviour is that it is *ambiguous*. People on the receiving end obtain a mixed message that the other person is willing to go along with the task or situation but seems unhappy at some level. When approached directly about this suspected discontent, these individuals will usually respond by saying, 'Oh, it's OK', whilst feeling resentful that the other person wasn't sufficiently sensitive to perceive their true needs. Think of a small child who pushes you away in anger but desperately wants a cuddle.

What to do when confronted with passive-aggressive behaviour: If the person you are dealing with is manifesting any of the behaviours I have described, it might be worth trying some of the following strategies:

- Similar to passive individuals, consider that this person may suffer from low self-esteem in spite of their outward appearance of confidence. Again, consider your choice of words carefully so that you don't run the risk of being seen as punishing or critical.
- It's also worth taking into account that although *you* may want to 'clear the air' and have a full and frank discussion, this person will avoid confrontation at all costs and either agree with you (and secretly resent you whilst seeking to sabotage your suggestions) or become withdrawn and stonewall you altogether.
- Try to bolster their self-esteem by complimenting their work and showing appreciation for any contributions they have made.
- If you are working with them or they are working for you, try to make the process seem as collaborative as possible and reward any positive inputs they might provide.

Aggressive behaviour

Many people have learned to use an overtly aggressive style of behaviour from childhood onwards and have often found this to be a successful strategy for getting their own way with others. Because this bullying style of behaviour is often rewarded through the compliance of others, it becomes reinforced or 'hard-wired' into the individual's way of operating within the world. Aggressive people can often be *narcissistic*, believing that they are special in some way and better than others. They may lack empathy, which is the ability to see things from the point of view of others (unless it's to sense their weaknesses and exploit them), and they also maintain beliefs like 'win at all costs or others will take advantage of you'. Aggressive people frequently experience difficulty in managing their anger and are given to outbursts of rage or, in extreme examples, acts of physical violence.

Of all the *unhelpful negative emotions* listed in Chapter 1, anger is the most seductive and addictive (Goleman, 1996). This is because it triggers huge amounts of adrenaline and can make the individual feel fearless and powerful when faced with a conflict of opinion. Other unhelpful negative emotions, such as anxiety, guilt, depression and so on, have a tendency to make us feel vulnerable. Anger, on the other hand, can make us feel invulnerable because, as a survival mechanism, it subdues our left pre-frontal cortex—the rational, reflective part of our brains—and ignites the *amygdala*, our internal controller for primitive 'fight or flight' survival responses (LeDoux, 1992).

Paradoxically, anger and aggressive behaviour can be a response to fear. I have worked with many offenders and managed the provision of career counselling in London prisons. Haven spoken to a number of male offenders, many admitted to feelings of anxiety on the wings and the perceived need to appear tough at all times, because to appear vulnerable would mark them out as a potential victim. These individuals were understandably hypervigilant for any signs of 'disrespect' from other prisoners, which they evaluated as a potential threat. As you can imagine, this creates a volatile situation with hundreds of anxious, incarcerated men walking around acting tough and perceiving the very behaviour they are using to defend themselves as a threat from others. Unfortunately, this often leads male prisoners to switch from anxiety to anger in a split second and deliver a pre-emptive attack to 'get their defence in first' (Hollin, 2005; Bekowitz, 1986).

The downside of aggressive behaviour: Whilst many people who adopt this style of behaviour gain short-term advantages through getting their own way by dominating others, in the medium to long term this strategy acts against them. The biblical saying, 'live by the sword, die by the sword' (Matthew 26:52, King James Bible) holds true for these individuals because although people may comply with their demands out of fear, they will inevitably harbour resentment and take revenge if an opportunity presents itself. This leads to a vicious cycle of *negative reciprocity*, where one individual may 'win' the encounter through aggressive behaviour but sow the seeds for retribution, leading to further conflict. Very often, individuals with an aggressive style of behaviour feel slightly paranoid between encounters as they sense others' resentment towards them. All of these processes consume huge amounts of emotional energy and can lead to long-term health consequences such as high blood pressure, a dangerous condition that can put the individual at risk of stroke (Mental Health Foundation, 2008).

Ultimately, success in the workplace depends on cultivating mutually beneficial, positive relationships, and it takes a great deal of time and energy to cultivate these. Stephen Covey (1999) likens this to making deposits in an *emotional bank account* with others. Each time you show courtesy and consideration, you make a deposit – even if there is a difference of opinion. Aggression and all the behaviours that flow from it lead to a massive withdrawal and, frequently, 'bankruptcy' in terms of the relationship.

What to do when confronted with aggressive behaviour: It stands to reason that if you feel yourself to be in danger of physical threat, you need to withdraw from the situation as quickly as possible and enlist the support of others. I want to help you to deal with situations in the workplace where the attacks are verbal rather than physical:

- Evaluate the power balance in this exchange and consider whether you are at a disadvantage. It may be distasteful to walk away from this type of situation, but confronting someone who has power over you within the workplace can have negative consequences. Think about your options: are there witnesses who will support you in making a formal complaint at a later stage? Remember, actively withdrawing from an aggressively confrontational situation can be an act of assertiveness, particularly if the other person has lost control of their emotions.
- Try to take a deep breath and remain as calm as possible. This will activate your *parasympathetic nervous system* (PNS), which is responsible for self-soothing. Remember, the other person's *sympathetic nervous system* (SNS) has been fired up by their anger and their rational left prefrontal cortex is shutting down while they rant, so that they are not thinking with any clarity whatsoever.
- If you have an 'exploder' on your hands, the best strategy is to say nothing or very little. This leaves them with no place to go and eventually they will fizzle out. Verbal outbursts consume a huge amount of energy and can't be sustained for long periods. If they start up again after a brief pause, stand back and wait patiently for the next surge of wrath to subside.
- Do not, under any circumstances, give in to the temptation to fight fire with fire and counter with aggression. They're pumped up with adrenaline and want a fight. If you let them provoke you into uncontrolled anger, you'll lose your rational advantage and the moral high ground.
- If they have calmed down sufficiently, ask them what *specifically* their grievance is and then offer to sit down and discuss it with them. If they continue to remain highly aroused, suggest discussing

the matter at a later stage and calmly withdraw from the situation. Congratulate yourself for acting with restraint and dignity.

What I have just described is the interpersonal equivalent to practising *aikido*. Aikido is a Japanese martial art developed in the nineteenth century. One of its main principles involves gently deflecting the force of your attacker rather than meeting in head on. It also emphasises self-control, highly useful in any confrontational situation.

Learning assertiveness skills

Having completed the questionnaire at the start of the section, you will hopefully be able to determine where you are across the following spectrum:

PASSIVE ⟶ ASSERTIVE ⟶ AGGRESSIVE

Most of us could do with some improvement to our assertiveness skills in the workplace; a good starting point is to use the *ABCDE formulation* method you learned in Chapter 1 to analyse typical situations in which you would benefit from being more assertive.

A
Consider these typical *activating events* (A):

- Interdepartmental meetings
- Performance reviews
- Supervisory meetings
- Interactions with other colleagues
- Work-related social events (office parties, drinks after work)

B
What type of *beliefs* (B) about the situation do you hold when you fail to assert yourself or act in an aggressive manner?

'I hate confrontations and conflict. If I stand up for myself I'll be overwhelmed by anxiety and won't be able to cope.'
'If I try to assert myself it could lead to a row and the others losing their tempers. I'll get the blame and everyone will feel bad.'
'It's taken me a long time to be accepted by the group. If I upset anyone by voicing my opinions, I may be ostracised.'
'Arguments always have a negative outcome – there's always one winner and one loser (usually me).'

Or:

'I'm won't take crap from anyone.'
'I *should* be respected by others and they need to show it.'
'If I don't win the argument/get my own way, it's a sign of weakness.'
'If I use anger, I'll get my own way.'
'If I bottle up my anger, it'll damage my health. I need to get it out of my system.'

C

Reflect on the negative behavioural and emotional *consequences* (C) leading from your beliefs about the situation:

- Passive behaviour leading to temporary relief followed by a sense of failure.
- 'People pleasing' (putting the needs of others first at your expense) followed by resentment.
- Never getting your voice heard at meetings and feeling frustrated.

Or:

- An immediate feeling of self-righteousness and power after the expression of anger followed by guilt or shame.
- People avoiding you after a heated exchange and the need to 'build bridges' and repair the relationship.
- Feelings of physical exhaustion or other symptoms of stress.
- The habit of being aggressive at work becomes 'hard-wired' and starts to have a corrosive effect on your personal life as you find yourself losing your temper with loved ones at the slightest provocation.

D and E

Having identified typical unhelpful *beliefs* that get activated in interpersonal exchanges with others, the next step is to *dispute* (D) these unhelpful beliefs to obtain *effective new thinking* (E) that will enable you to assert yourself in future situations.

'I *can* tolerate strong emotions and function – I manage in other situations. It's worth breaking through the fear barrier to get my point across. Even if I just try, I'll feel better about myself afterwards.'

'What's the worst thing that could happen if I put my views forward and the others disagree? At least they'll respect me for having an opinion rather than sitting on the fence all the time.'

'I've got every right to get my point across in a reasonable way. Working relationships are all about compromise, not a nil-sum game of win or lose.'

Or:
'Perhaps I'm seeing threats to my position where they don't exist. Controlling my temper is a greater sign of strength than losing it.'

'I get my own way in the short term because I intimidate people, but they probably dislike me rather than respect me. If I'm direct and straightforward, they'll think more of me.'

'If I keep getting angry all the time, I'll risk getting high blood pressure and suffer a stroke. I can find more active ways to let off steam rather than ranting at people.'

You might find it helpful to record your effective new thinking on a cue card to remind yourself of these insights when you are about to enter a situation in which you need to assert yourself.

Putting assertiveness into practice

Now it's time to set yourself some assertiveness goals at work in order to develop confidence in this domain. If you find yourself procrastinating, bear in mind that you will feel better after you've taken action rather than avoiding the situation. It's a bit like avoiding a visit to the dentist when you have toothache: some short-term discomfort will lead to long-term relief. In general, there are two types of situations in which to practice assertive behaviour.

Planned assertiveness: In this situation you have the luxury of planning what you are going to say to the other person. For example, you may have arranged to meet with the other person and given them a broad idea about what you want to discuss. Your key advantage is that you rehearse (or even script) the points you want to make in an assertive but nonaggressive manner. What you need to be aware of is the tendency to worry about the outcome or make yourself angry, so that you'll end up thinking and acting in less than helpful ways at the meeting. Remember to *dispute* any unhelpful thoughts and rehearse your *effective new thinking* – above all, remind yourself that it will be *unfortunate but not awful* if things don't go your way. The main thing is that you will have practised being assertive and will be able to learn from the outcome to further refine your skills.

Unplanned assertiveness: You may find yourself in a situation that suddenly becomes adversarial without any chance of preparing your response in advance. This could typically include thoughtless behaviour from a colleague that you find annoying, unfair criticism of your work or conduct or aggressive point scoring by others at meetings. The obvious downside of this situation is that you won't have any time to prepare your response in a calm environment. However, the advantage is that you also won't have time to brood on the situation and risk making yourself worried or angry. The key thing you need to decide in advance is that whenever these situations arise, take a deep breath, pause and behave in a calm manner *even if you don't feel this way*. Essentially this is using the 'acting as if' technique I outlined in Chapter 2. The chances are that if you slow yourself down and *act* in a calm way, you will *think* and *feel* calmer. You will also show others that you are unperturbed and unlikely to be intimidated by their behaviour.

The following *cognitive* and *behavioural* techniques will help you to assert yourself in even the most challenging situations.

Assertiveness toolkit

Use your eyes

Even if you are feeling nervous, it's essential that you maintain good eye contact with the other person because it will give them the impression that you are confident in your position and you have full conviction in the points you are making. If you find yourself feeling generally awkward in making eye contact with people, keep practising in every social interaction. Some aggressive or manipulative individuals will try to dominate the social interaction with their eyes by trying to 'outstare' you. Don't let this disconcert you: maintain a calm and even gaze at all times. Conversely, if you become emotionally aroused, try to avoid aggressively 'eyeballing' the other person as this will simply escalate the situation.

Be clear in your communication

Try to summarise, with as much clarity as possible, the key points you want to convey to the other person. This process will engage your left prefrontal cortex (the rational, decision making part of your brain);

this will in turn have a calming effect on your right prefrontal cortex, which has a stronger connection to your emotional 'fight or flight' sub-cortical areas (Siegel, 2013). You can strengthen this analytical trigger by jotting down a few notes if you have the opportunity. Using this method will keep the exchange focussed and also pre-empt any attempts by the other person to sidetrack the key issues you want to get across.

Speak reasonably slowly and don't waver from your key points

Communicate at a calm and even pace so that the other person has every chance of hearing what you want to get across. You can also influence the dynamics of the interaction if the situation has become quite heated. If you persist in speaking with a calm voice and at a slow tempo, the other person may begin to unconsciously mimic your behaviour as their emotional arousal level starts to decline. It's a bit like playing soothing music to someone who is angry or upset. It is vitally important that you resist any temptation to rush through your points because you are feeling nervous and want to 'get it over and done with'. Equally, if you become angry, there is a risk that your key points will become an incomprehensible barrage aimed at the other person. As I mentioned, if you speak slowly and calmly, you are more likely to look and feel confident. If the other person tries to lead you off in different directions, use the 'stuck record' technique: calmly and repeatedly return to the point you are making until it has been resolved to your satisfaction.

Keep your anger in check

Anger is seductive! It may *feel* more empowering to displace anxiety with aggression but you're far more likely to trigger an aggressive or other highly emotional response in the other person, which will lead to a breakdown in communication and a failure to resolve your issues. If you do feel angry, try to channel this energy into being firm and emphatic with the other person rather than acting in an aggressive manner. The other problem with anger is that it has a negative impact on left prefrontal cortex rational thinking and will compromise your ability to communicate optimally. If you remain calm and act in a firm manner, you will increase the chances of the other person treating your points of view with respect and giving them careful consideration.

Take responsibility for your thoughts, feelings and actions

What I mean by this is that you want to avoid making *global statements*. An example of this could be a recent situation in which your boss said something about your work at a meeting that you weren't happy about. If you were to say, 'You're *always* criticising me in team meetings,' your communication would be unhelpfully ambiguous. It's far more helpful to be as specific as possible about a grievance or issue you want resolved. Let's say the other party acted in a certain way and you felt hurt or angry in response. You need to draw attention to what they said or did specifically and how you *interpreted* their actions. This makes it clear that you are taking responsibility for your thoughts and feelings about the situation, because there is a chance that you may have misunderstood the other person's intentions. This offers them the possibility of clarifying their intentions rather than backing them into a corner with a global statement. So instead of saying, 'You're *always* criticising me,' you could offer, 'When you said my financial projections for next year were sloppy in front of the whole team, I thought that it undermined my authority and we could have discussed the issue in private.' Here are a few examples.

Unhelpful global statements:

- 'You just couldn't care less about all of the sacrifices I've made for the team.'
- 'All this company thinks about is profit margins and never takes staff opinions into account.'
- 'I've just about had enough of the way you treat me.'
- 'You patronise me in front of everyone.'

Helpful specific statements:

- 'When this branch introduced a policy of late and weekend opening for customers without any staff consultation, my impression was that colleagues' opinions on child care difficulties hadn't been listened to.'
- 'When you gave me feedback at my annual performance appraisal review, I don't think you took into account the fact that I've increased revenue for the division over the last two months.'
- 'I wanted to draw your attention to the way you behave when we approach project deadlines. You have a tendency to shout at me and I feel nervous as a result. I then find it hard to concentrate and get the work completed on time.'

Make your point and let the other person respond

As I mentioned previously, controlling your breathing is one of the best ways of regulating emotional arousal, particularly for situations in which you experience anxiety or anger. After you have made your point, pause and take a deep, steady breath. This will soothe your nerves by activating your parasympathetic nervous system (PNS) and increase the flow of oxygen to your brain, helping you to think with greater clarity. It will also give the person that you are communicating with the opportunity to take in what you have just said, reflect on the content of your statement and frame a response. It's vitally important for you to make sure that each point is resolved, as much as possible, before making your next point. Try to avoid any inclination to fire off your points in quick succession in order to make yourself heard while the other person is giving you 'air time'. If you do this there is a risk that both of you will lose track of the key issues you want resolved.

Increase your confidence by practising assertiveness regularly

Sparring with a partner, or *kumite* ('free-fighting'), is an important part of practising karate and yet many practitioners avoid this activity due to a lack of confidence. The hard truth of the matter is that in order to become confident in karate sparring, you have to actually practice sparring at every opportunity. The same holds true of practising assertive behaviour–you need to go outside of your comfort zone regularly. Try to practice the assertiveness skills I've described in situations that you would normally find challenging but not completely overwhelming. This might include situations in which you would normally avoid asserting yourself because the situation triggers anxiety or anger and you may believe that you won't be able to communicate effectively whilst experiencing these emotions. As with all *behavioural experiments* in CBT, you will gather evidence that nothing really bad happens when you assert yourself, leading to a virtuous cycle of increased confidence and the practice of assertiveness in more challenging situations.

Always bear in mind that assertiveness is a skill, like any other, and its execution becomes easier with regular practice, even though you may experience some nervousness or annoyance when exercising these skills. Tolerating emotional discomfort is a tiny price to pay for the amount of confidence, patience and increased resilience you stand to gain. Even if you walk away from the situation without achieving your desired outcome, the very fact that you have asserted yourself will help to make you feel as though you are more in control at work, and feeling in control is a sure-fire way of reducing stress and increasing your sense of autonomy. I will now go on to consider ways in which you can influence others in the workplace by establishing positive rapport.

Establishing rapport with others

Using empathy

One of the most important interpersonal qualities needed to develop rapport with others is *empathy*. This is the ability to enter the other person's world as you interact with them and to try as much as possible to see things from their perspective. When you communicate with someone else empathically, it is like a meeting of two minds and is perhaps one of the highest forms of communication as it requires you to create a mental representation of how the other person perceives you and the situation. It also requires you to tune in to how they are feeling *emotionally* by allowing yourself to experience what they are feeling right now, whether it is calm, joy, enthusiasm, anger, frustration or anxiety. People often confuse empathy for *sympathy* or *compassion*. Although it's possible to feel either of these emotions when you empathise with someone, it's not essential – you can even *dislike* the other person. The main thing you are trying to achieve is to see things from their perspective, regardless of how you feel about them personally. Practising empathy definitely isn't 'woolly' of 'fluffy' – the most effective torturers are highly empathic (Egan, 2002). An empathic torturer doesn't put a gun to your head; they put a gun against your child's head because they know exactly how you will feel. Empathy is practiced in a wide range of contexts, from caring occupations, such as counselling, to sales and management professions. It is an essential life skill both within and outside of the workplace because, practiced effectively, empathy lays the foundation for building and maintaining professional, personal and intimate relationships. But how do you become more effective in practising empathy?

Listen

Part of my practice as a CBT therapist requires me to work with couples whose relationships have run into difficulty. In some cases the individuals concerned are using therapy to decide whether or not to separate. Depending on the dynamics of the relationship and personalities of the couple, the sessions can be highly volatile with a great deal of shouting and accusations flying back and forth or emotionally flat with an air of hopelessness. One of the first things I do with couples is to teach both parties communication skills. They are asked to take turns and simply listen to their partner as they describe how they feel about the relationship, and then check that they have understood where the other person is coming from. I used to feel slightly self-conscious when imposing this task on highly intelligent and apparently successful couples, particularly when their body language and facial expressions told me that they found the task rather patronising. However, in most cases even the most intelligent and sophisticated individuals struggled with this task because instead of actively listening, they were mentally preparing a response including the points *they* wanted to make.

If you want to enter into the other person's mind and see the world from their perspective, you have to temporarily suspend your own ego. Try to really tune into the content of what they are saying, their body language, facial expressions, the tonality and pace of their voice. What messages are you receiving at both an intellectual and emotional level? It is also really important to adopt a *nonjudgemental* stance. Forget your agenda for the moment and don't allow any preconceived ideas about the person or the situation to distort your perspective. If you allow these tendencies to creep in, you run the risk of *mind reading*, which we encountered in Chapter 1. Try instead to let each moment unfold as you listen to the other person, constantly projecting yourself into their mind and experiencing what they are thinking and feeling.

Check your understanding

After you have given the other person your full attention and an opportunity to present their point of view, it's vital that you clarify your understanding of what they have just said. It's often helpful to present your 'working hypothesis' tentatively and offer the other person the opportunity to clarify any misunderstanding on your part. You can do this by briefly *summarising* what you consider to be the main points that the other person has just communicated. Preface your summary with a statement like, 'It seems to me that...' and conclude with a question, such as, 'Have I got that right?'

Sometimes the other person may communicate more through body language and facial expression than the content of what they are saying. In fact, there may seemingly be a contradiction between the two (e.g. they're agreeing on a course of action that you're proposing, but they look very unhappy). This type of situation requires a very delicate approach and you might gently offer a clarification like, 'I may be wrong but I get the sense that...' and wait to see what response you elicit before going further.

Create the conditions for empathy and rapport

Body language and nonverbal communication are very important aspects in developing rapport. There are many checklists available that provide generic instructions on which postures to adopt and techniques for mirroring the other person's gestures. The problem with adopting these approaches is that they don't feel genuine when you practice them in social interactions and you also run the risk of being perceived as manipulative by the other person. However, it's worth *adjusting* your style of communication depending on the context of the situation and the personality of the individual you are dealing with. For example, if you are naturally extroverted and exuberant in your communication, but the other person is apparently introverted and speaks in a tentative, quiet manner, it would be advisable to adjust the volume and speed of your voice and your physical gestures within a *similar range* to that of the other person, without faking a set of behaviours that are incongruent with your personality. Conversely, if you're considerate and reflective in the way you communicate and you're interacting with someone who has a highly enthusiastic, upbeat style, you may need to go up a gear but within the range of what feels natural to you.

A very subtle and often overlooked aspect for creating a sense of empathy and rapport is to listen very carefully to the type of *language* the other person is using. If you concentrate, you may hear them use images and turns of phrase that fall into the following categories:

- Visual: 'I see what you mean'; 'I don't see it like that'
- Auditory: 'I hear what you're saying'; 'Listen to this'
- Kinaesthetic: 'I feel as though'; 'My gut reaction is'

According to the educational theorist David Kolb (1984), we develop preferred learning styles in childhood and absorb knowledge more effectively when information is conveyed visually, aurally or kinaesthetically depending on our individual learning style. These learning styles continue into adulthood so that visual learners respond better to written words, pictures and graphs. Auditory learners obviously pay close attention to the spoken word, whilst kinaesthetic learners may need to move around and use props like a flip chart or Post-it Notes. If you notice that the other person is using a predominantly visual, auditory or kinaesthetic style of language, you may increase rapport by enhancing your communication with different methods in line with their preferred modality. At the most basic level, you could simply adopt their preferred terminology and illustrate your points using visual, auditory or kinaesthetic imagery. This will increase the likelihood of the other person feeling that you truly understand them.

One of the most important needs we have as human beings is to feel understood and validated at some level. That's why good listeners, counsellors and psychotherapists are in constant demand. Stephen Covey (1999) refers to meeting this need in others as providing 'psychological air'. If you are able to make the other person feel understood, you stand a good chance of building rapport with them. Even if you disagree about the matter in hand on this occasion, you will have made a valuable emotional investment in the relationship and sown the seeds for a positive interaction when you next meet.

If you forget everything else I've taught you in this chapter, remember this:

1 Emotional intelligence can often lead to greater success in the workplace than technical expertise.
2 Even if you *feel* nervous in social situations, it doesn't mean that you *appear* nervous.
3 Focus on the other person during social interactions rather than your own performance.
4 If you avoid emotional discomfort by failing to assert yourself, your self-esteem will suffer in the long term.
5 Assertiveness is a skill that becomes easier with regular practice.
6 Empathy is perhaps one of the highest forms of communication. It requires you to create a mental representation of how the other person perceives you and the situation.

References

American Psychiatric Association. (2013). *The diagnostic and statistical manual of mental disorders, Fifth Edition (DSM-5)*. American Psychiatric Publishing.
Bible: *King James Version*. (2011). Collins.
Clark, D.M. and Wells, A. (1995). A cognitive model of social phobia. In R. Heimberg, M. Liebowitz, D.A. Hope and F.R. Schneier (Eds), *Social phobia: diagnosis, assessment and treatment*. Guilford Press.
Covey, S. (1999). *The 7 habits of highly effective people*. Simon Schuster.
Egan, G. (2002). *The skilled helper*. Brooks/Cole.

Golding, W. (1954). *Lord of the flies*. Penguin Group US.

Goleman, D. (1996). *Emotional intelligence*. Bloomsbury Publishing.

Grimm, J. and Grimm, W. (2014). *The original folk and fairy tales of the brothers grimm*. Translated by Jack Zipes. Deckle Edge.

Hartmann, L.M. (1983). A meta-cognitive model of social anxiety: implications for treatment. *Clinical Psychology Review*, 3: 435–56.

Hastings, S. (2004). Emotional intelligence. Published in the Times Educational Supplement, October 15, 2004.

Hollin, C.R. (2005). *The essential handbook of offender assessment and treatment*. Wiley.

King, S. (2013). *Carrie*. Hodder Paperbacks.

Kolb, D.A. (1984). *Experiential learning: experience as the source of learning and development*. Prentice Hall.

Leary, M.R. (2001). Social anxiety as an early warning system: a refinement and extension of the self-presentation theory of social anxiety. In S.G. Hoffmann and P.M. DiBartolo (Eds), *From social anxiety to social phobia: multiple perspectives* (pp. 321–334). Allyn and Bacon.

LeDoux, J. (1992). Emotion and the limbic system concept, *Concepts in Neuroscience*, 2, 1992.

Mental Health Foundation. (2008). Boiling point: anger and what we can do about it.

Murphy, P. and Hoff Oberlin, L. (2005). *Overcoming passive aggression: how to stop hidden anger from spoiling your relationships, career and happiness*. Da Capo Long Life.

Siegel, D. (2013). *Mindsight*. Oneworld Publications.

Young, J.E. and Klosko, J.S. (1994). *Reinventing your life*. Plume.

Chapter 7

Using cognitive and behavioural approaches for increased energy and self care

The world of work in the twenty-first century is developing at a dizzyingly faster pace with each passing year, and although this can be exhilarating, even if you are fortunate enough to love your career, the demands on your mental and physical energy can take their toll. This final chapter will help you to identify the early warning signs of potential burnout and give you a range of different approaches to prevent it from happening in the first place.

Be aware of the danger signs of work-related stress

The danger signs of work-related stress can be quite subtle and build up over a long period of time. As such, they can often go unnoticed until they become a major problem, so it's worth paying particular attention to the symptoms outlined in this chapter. You need to be particularly vigilant for any decline in your physical and mental well-being. Take note of minor ailments such as constant headaches and colds, muscular pains such as back and neck ache and stomach problems such as excessive acidity or irritable bowels. It's tempting to try and fix the problem with over-the-counter medication and power on at work, and that's fine as a temporary solution. But if symptoms persist over the course of a few weeks, you really need to think about what the underlying cause might be. Think of your body as a barometer to your overall well-being. What is it trying to tell you? If minor aliments persist, this is often a sign that your immune system is not functioning optimally, which is one of the first signs of prolonged stress. It you continue to ignore these warning signs, you run the risk of developing more serious health problems.

As we have seen throughout this book, the mind and body interact with one another in complex ways, so that if your physical health deteriorates, it will have an impact on your mental health and vice versa. Paying attention to your psychological well-being is essential but often overlooked because it's easier to spot physical illnesses. Two of the most common responses to work-related stress are symptoms of depression and/or anxiety. When considering whether you are suffering from depression, you need to ask yourself the following questions:

- Are you taking less interest or pleasure in things that you would normally enjoy?
- Are you suffering from low mood and also a sense of hopelessness ('what's the point')?
- Do you find it difficult getting to sleep at night, waking up in the early hours, or conversely, sleeping far more than usual?
- Has your energy declined and do you feel tired all the time?
- Have you gone off your food, or conversely, do you constantly comfort eat to improve your mood?
- Do you feel like a failure or that you've let yourself or other people down?
- Has your ability to concentrate for extended periods deteriorated?
- Do you find yourself moving more slowly than usual, or the opposite, being fidgety, restless and moving about all the time?

If you've experienced these symptoms for several days over the past fortnight, you're probably going through a rough patch and need to take better care of yourself. If these problems have occurred more than half the days or every day over the last two weeks, this is a serious indication that you need to seek professional help, starting with your doctor. One of the key warning signs of depression is any thought that you would be better off dead or of harming yourself in some way. If you ever find yourself making actual plans to end your life, *get help immediately*!

Let's consider the symptoms of anxiety:

- Do you feel nervous, anxious or on edge?
- Do you find it hard to stop worrying or control your worries?
- Do you find yourself worrying excessively about different things?
- Do you find it hard to relax?
- Are you so restless that you find it hard to sit still?
- Do you get annoyed or irritable more easily than usual?
- Are you afraid that something awful might happen?

Measuring the level of severity of these symptoms is the same process as for depression. If you've experienced these problems over a fortnight, the level of severity can be defined according to their frequency as low (several days), moderate (more than half the days) or severe (nearly every day).

Both sets of questions derive from two diagnostic tools that are widely used by mental health professionals throughout the UK National Health Service: the Patient Health Questionnaire (PHQ9) (Kroenke et al., 2001) and the Generalized Anxiety Disorder (GAD7) Questionnaire (Spitzer et al., 2006). We all suffer from periods of low mood or increased anxiety from time to time, but you can use the above checklists to take stock of how severe the problem is – if they're good enough for health care professionals, they're good enough for you.

It's vitally important to take action if your mood deteriorates or your anxiety levels increase persistently over time, because these emotional problems have a tendency to feed off themselves so that they become increasingly difficult to break free from. Depression depletes energy, leading to a consequent reduction in activity. This is referred to in psychological parlance as a *lethargy cycle*, a downward spiral in which the individual does less, has less energy as a result and does even less. This lack of activity leaves plenty of time for *ruminating* or brooding on one's problems, leading to a further darkening of mood. Increased anxiety has a similar maintenance cycle in that it leads people to avoid situations they perceive to be stressful, for example attending meetings or public speaking. As we've seen in Chapter 4, this intolerance of uncertainty shrinks the individual's comfort zone every time they avoid a challenging situation, furthering a downward spiral of reduced self-confidence. Prevention is better than cure, so if you're not already doing so, you need to invest time in a range of self-care activities that will inoculate you against stress in the workplace and life in general.

Look after yourself

Fitness wins

Most types of physical exercise offer stress-busting benefits like reduced blood pressure and increase in stamina. Physical activity also acts like an antidepressant by triggering a number of mood enhancing drugs in the brain, such as endorphins and serotonin. Remember, also, what we learned about *flow* in Chapter 3: if you're fully absorbed in a physical activity, you get a mental holiday from all of your cares. In addition to improving mood and general levels of physical fitness, exercise improves brain power by getting more oxygen to your grey matter, so you'll be mentally sharper the next day. Choose an activity that suits your lifestyle and fitness level, preferably one that you will enjoy to maintain motivation. An ideal fitness programme combines aerobic activity, muscle resistance training and gentle stretching for all around physical well-being. You don't have to be an athlete – just increasing the amount of time you spend walking can do wonders for your health. Regular walking can reduce the risk of heart disease, type 2 diabetes, stroke, asthma and certain cancers (NHS, 2014). Other top tips for improving your physical health include:

- **Cut down on the booze**. The NHS recommends that men shouldn't drink more than 3–4 units per day and women 2–3 units. Also, three nights of abstinence each week is highly recommended to clear the liver. Although alcohol is enjoyable in small quantities, it's also a highly addictive drug that wrecks lives. Every time you have a drink, the pleasure centres in your brain light up like a pinball machine (the same process is activated by street drugs like cocaine, gambling and even shopping). That's why the call to the bar is so seductive.
- **Improve nutrition**. Getting a balanced diet including fresh fruit, vegetables and foods rich in omega 3 will boost your physical and mental functioning. It's also worth cutting back on processed carbohydrates (e.g. bread, pasta) as their consumption increases blood glucose and subsequent insulin levels, making it harder to reduce body fat (Sisson, 2012). A Greek fisherman once told me, 'Don't eat what you can't burn'. Given that he was in his nineties and still fishing, it seemed to have worked for him.
- **Cut down on caffeine and drink more water**. Without wishing to sound censorious, caffeine, along with alcohol, is a drug, albeit less harmful. In addition to coffee, caffeine can be found in tea, chocolate, energy drinks and over-the-counter medication such as flu and cold remedies. Moderate consumption is fine, but caffeine acts on the central nervous system, so if you experience palpitations or difficulty relaxing or sleeping, you should reduce your consumption. I routinely ask patients I'm treating for anxiety about their caffeine intake and they're often amazed to find that switching to decaf makes the problem go away. Water, on the other hand, should be consumed throughout the day to maintain optimum levels of mental and physical energy. The European Food Safety Authority recommends that men should drink a minimum of 2.0 litres of fluid per day and women 1.6 litres (EFSA, 2010).

Strive for a work-life balance

If you're serious about your career, it's all too easy to give work central importance in your life to the exclusion of other domains like family, friends and leisure pursuits. Some people are so invested in their careers that they find work addictive and experience difficulty withdrawing from it for even the briefest period. However, if you don't take regular breaks to 'sharpen the saw' as Stephen Covey (1999) says, the mental and physical pressures will eventually take their toll. You don't have to spend a fortune travelling. Any enjoyable activity that gives you a break from work can be recuperative if it provides your mind and body respite from your day-to-day duties. Don't just use weekends and holidays to obtain balance; weave regular breaks into your daily routine. It's often tempting to work through your lunch break, particularly if you're under pressure and working to deadlines. But if you constantly keep your foot on the accelerator, sooner or later you'll run out of energy and your productivity will decline.

Connect with others

As human beings, we are social creatures and thrive in the company of others. In fact, maintaining positive relationships is highly important for psychological well-being and social isolation contributes significantly to depression. Relationships require constant nurturing and need to be guarded from the insidious effects of overworking or stress at work. Even if you're having a stressful time, try to leave your problems in the workplace and don't allow them to contaminate your relationships with others. It's OK to seek support and discuss your concerns occasionally, but if you constantly use others to 'get things off your chest', you risk placing a strain on the relationship. Even if they are happy to hear your tales of woe, going over these things repeatedly won't help you because all you're doing is engaging in verbal rumination, which will bring your mood down. If you are spending time with your partner, family or friends, try to be fully present. Every time you find your mind wandering back to your concerns at work, notice this and gently bring your attention back to the other person.

Invest in yourself

Whatever your chosen occupation, try to constantly perfect your craft through continuous professional development. Attend training courses that will enrich your skills and read around your area of expertise to deepen your knowledge. If you fail to invest in yourself, you risk getting stuck in a rut and your work will become less enjoyable and stale. The majority of us spend most of our adult lives in the workplace. You owe it to yourself to make the experience as positive as possible.

My final piece of advice for improving your psychological well-being is the regular practice of some form of meditation to decrease stress and optimise cognitive functioning. I will share with you a practice that, although ancient in origin, is fast becoming a worldwide phenomenon because of the growing evidence base for its efficacy in promoting psychological well-being.

Mindfulness

Most modern-day careers place increasing demands on our mental as well as physical energy. If we don't replenish our cognitive resources on a regular basis, they will inevitably become depleted. Try thinking of the way you use your mind and emotions as the tools of your trade. Each day you are probably involved in some type of analytical thinking process (e.g. problem solving) and managing or utilising your emotions (empathising with colleagues, maintaining your motivation). If you were a mechanic and neglected to maintain your tools adequately, eventually they would let you down and you wouldn't be able to do your job. Your mind and emotions require a similar level of care and attention to enable you to achieve well-being and success in your work and personal life. Stephen Covey refers to this type of personal maintenance as the seventh habit of highly effective people (Covey, 1999): 'sharpen the saw'.

One of the best ways of replenishing your mental resources is to practice some form of meditation, which provides a refuge for our busy minds and the emotional turbulence we experience from the stress of modern living. There are many types of meditational practice and you may wish to research what's available to you locally depending on your personal preferences. Also, meditation doesn't have to be practised within a spiritual context and can be used as a method for achieving calm by people of all faiths without conflicting with their religious beliefs. It's also used widely within the corporate world as a means of achieving mental clarity. Steve Jobs, Apple's founder and former chief executive, practised Zen Buddhism and told his biographer Walter Isaacson that the calm he achieved through meditation allowed his intuition to blossom (Isaacson, 2011). *Mindfulness meditation* is one such example and is attaining a huge number of practitioners worldwide because of its simplicity and effectiveness. It is also used with patients as a treatment for anxiety and depression within the British National Health Service because of its clinical evidence base.

What is mindfulness?

Mindfulness meditation was originally adapted from the ancient Buddhist practice of Vipassana meditation. What is absolutely amazing is that although the practice of meditation is at least 5,000 years old, cutting-edge technology is enabling us to see its beneficial effects on the brain for the first time – something its practitioners intuited and for which there is now empirical evidence. An example of this is data obtained from the brain scans of a group of meditating Buddhist monks. The results showed that, if practised regularly, meditation can enable the mind to be calm and free from turbulent emotions such as anger and anxiety (Lutz et al., 2004).

The popularity of mindfulness owes a great deal to Dr. Jon Kabat-Zinn, who adapted its practice into *mindfulness based stress reduction* as a method for helping his patients to cope with chronic pain. This 'secular' adaptation of mindfulness has been expanded to many different approaches since Kabat-Zinn published his seminal work *Full Catastrophe Living* in 1990. These approaches range from clinical applications to prevent relapse into depression (*mindfulness based cognitive therapy*) to everyday practice by millions of people worldwide seeking to improve their mental well-being and cope with the demands of modern life. One of the central skills that mindfulness teaches us is the ability to focus our attention on the present moment – right here and now – without letting our minds wander to either future events that we anticipate or past events we have experienced. At this point I want to remind you of some of Mihaly Csikszentmihalyi's (2002) principles of *flow* that we encountered in Chapter 3. You may remember that Csikszentmihalyi asserted that without some form of training, most people find it difficult to focus their thoughts for more than a few minutes and that our mental default state is entropy – internal disorder.

Our minds drift backwards and forwards between past and future events and are seldom focussed on the present moment. As a result, we tend to engage in two very unhelpful activities: *worry* when our thoughts focus on the future and *rumination* when we think of negative past events. Engaging in mindfulness is very similar to the experience of *flow* in that it enables us to become absorbed in the present moment and provides us with respite from worry and rumination (Figure 7.1).

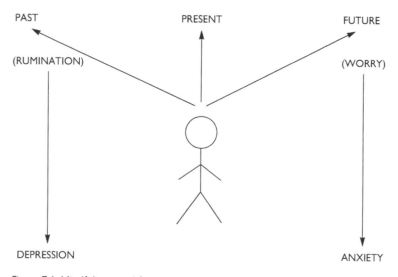

Figure 7.1 Mindfulness and focusing attention on the present moment.

Although the idea of focussing your attention on the present moment may sound easy and you may be thinking, 'Is that it?', attaining this focus is subtly challenging and requires understanding and regular practice. About 12 years ago I paid £500 each for my wife and I to learn transcendental meditation (TM), which is similar to mindfulness meditation. That was a lot of money and I had high expectations. We met our teacher in an office above a stationary shop in north London and he inducted us into the practice of TM separately. When it was my turn we engaged in a slightly esoteric ceremony in which I presented him with an item of fruit (a banana) and he chanted a number of incantations. After this he gave me my *mantra* and told me to keep repeating it, out loud and then silently in my head. It was at this point that I was asking myself, 'Is that it?', and becoming increasingly frustrated with my inability to focus my mind on the mantra. It was after a couple of sessions of weekly coaching with the teacher that I began to realise that the value for money came from the subtle tuition in how to gently bring my mind back to the present moment, and I've been practising ever since.

What I'd like you to do now is put down this book for a moment and focus on your surroundings. Spend the next few minutes focussing on what you can see, hear, touch, smell or taste.

How was that? How difficult was it for you to fully focus on your surroundings without some thoughts drifting into your consciousness and getting between you and your experience of the present moment? If you've practised the strategies I outlined in Chapter 5 on *focus*, you'll be aware of the mind's tendency to wander away from the present moment, even when you really want to be there. Have you ever neared the end of a holiday and found your mind wandering back to the work that awaits you when you return? You could be standing in front of the most beautiful sunset on earth but in your mind, you're back in the office worrying about all of the work that's piled up in your absence. Jon Kabat-Zinn described this in terms of incessant thoughts and feelings that act as constant obstacles to experiencing even the briefest moments of calm and contentment (Kabat-Zinn, 1990).

One of the potentially tragic flaws of human consciousness is that we risk drifting through our whole life only partially experiencing what is happening to us because our attention constantly wanders away from the present moment. As if this type of half-living wasn't bad enough, lack of focus on the present moment costs us a huge amount of mental and emotional energy. For example, if you are trying to write a report but your mind keeps wandering to the meeting you're due to attend later in the day or what you have to do in the evening, you are placing a number of simultaneous demands on your mind and depleting your glucose levels, as we learned from Baumeister in Chapter 4 (Baumeister and Tierney, 2011). So how can you become more adept at anchoring yourself to the present moment to fully experience the here and now *and* conserve your precious mental and emotional energy? I want to introduce you to the first steps of practising mindfulness.

If you've practised the *diaphragmatic breathing* exercises in Chapter 2 and the focussing techniques in Chapter 5, both of these approaches will stand you in good stead for the next exercise, which is aimed at calming your mind and strengthening your ability to focus on the present moment.

Step-by-step seated mindfulness practice

Step 1: Find a quiet place where you can escape from any disturbances, including telephone calls. I know that this can sometimes be a challenge but it's worth the effort. Increasingly we feel the need to be constantly available to others and might even feel guilt at the prospect of investing time in our own well-being. But if you don't attend to your own needs, you'll eventually become less effective in supporting others. Try to practise in the same place if you can. Make it your peaceful retreat so that by simply going there your brain associates this location with calmness. For optimum results the recommended amount of time to practise mindfulness is 15 minutes in the morning and evening. I know this seems like a big investment of your time, but many people find that practising mindfulness pays dividends. Even if you can only spare 5 minutes per day, begin with this and try to extend your practice gradually. Practising first thing in the morning is highly recommended as this will help you set the tone for the day by sending you out in a calm frame of mind. Just as a nutritious breakfast will increase your physical energy, practising meditation first thing in the morning will nourish your mind.

Step 2: Sit in a comfortable posture and try to keep your back straight and shoulders relaxed. Move slightly forward whilst remaining upright so that you avoid using the chair's backrest to support you. This will help you to focus on the rhythm of your breathing and prevent you from falling asleep when you become relaxed. Your aim is to enter a state of calm, focussing moment-by-moment on the unfolding present rather than dozing off. If you suffer from any kind of health problem (e.g. muscular or skeletal) that would cause you physical discomfort when adopting this posture, adapt this exercise so that you are able to practice in comfort.

Step 3: Next, close your eyes so that you can fully concentrate on your meditation without visual distractions. If, for whatever reason, you don't feel comfortable closing your eyes whilst meditating, you can obtain the same effect by focussing your eyes on a spot about 60 cm (2 ft) in front of you. It's very important for you to feel as safe as possible within your meditation environment. This is because our brains are hard-wired to continually scan the environment for potential threats (as usual, we've inherited this tendency from our ancient ancestors) even if we're not aware of this process at a conscious level (Raichle et al., 2001). By consciously acknowledging that you are safe in your current environment (or at least *safer*), you give your brain permission to reduce scanning for danger and focus its attention instead on attaining calm and relaxation. Whatever challenges there are in your life right now, try to think of putting them all in a box outside the room in which you are meditating. You can pick them up on the way out, but right now you need to take a break from them. Now that you're feeling safe and free from distractions, focus on *intent*. This is an important part of the process at the beginning of each session in which you state the intention to commit yourself fully to your meditation within the time available. This has the effect of focussing your internal resources on the task ahead.

Step 4: Now calmly focus attention on your breathing. Ideally you will be practising the deeper diaphragmatic breathing style I introduced you to in Chapter 2 rather than shallow chest breathing. Either way, let your breathing follow its own natural rhythm and begin to notice the subtle sensations of this physical process you normally take for granted. Notice, for instance, the slight coolness of the air as you breathe it in and how it feels slightly warmer when you exhale. Feel how soothing each breath is as it travels through your nose, down to your chest and stomach and then out again. With each inhalation you are gently activating your calming parasympathetic nervous system (PNS); with each exhalation you are ridding yourself of tension.

Step 5: Continue to pay attention to each inhalation and exhalation, that's all you have to do. When you notice your mind wandering, just bring your attention back to your breathing, having noted the thought and how it made you feel momentarily. If you find this process challenging at first, you could try counting each breath from one to ten and starting at the beginning again with each set. You will probably find yourself counting beyond ten or pursuing a thought that has entered your mind. Congratulate yourself on noticing this and bring your attention back to your breathing.

Step 6: You will probably notice the way your mind 'pulls' in different directions, chasing after thoughts that occur to you when your attention drifts away from each breath. If you are new to meditation, this level of activity within the mind during quiet moments may seem surprising, but it's actually quite normal. Your job is to notice these thoughts but avoid getting drawn into them, no matter how interesting they seem. On the other hand, whatever you do, don't try to block out your thoughts because this will result in a mental battle with yourself. Each time you notice a thought and then bring your attention back to your breath is the cognitive equivalent to lifting weights in the gym to develop muscle. By engaging in this subtle practice you are strengthening your focus of attention and developing neural pathways that will facilitate deeper relaxation and calm.

Step 7: Pay attention for any feelings of frustration and impatience that may occur while you are meditating, thoughts such as, 'Am I doing this right?', 'When am I going to feel relaxed?', 'Is there any point to this when I've got so many other things to do?'. These are very common reactions and they arise because we are conditioned to strive for an outcome in most domains of our life. Many people fall into the trap of starting meditation with the express aim of 'feeling calm' and they try very hard to relax and empty their mind, but become disappointed when their desired outcome doesn't materialise. This is because they are engaged in *thinking* rather than simply *being* in the moment. I know this may sound counterintuitive, but think about the last time you found it difficult to get to sleep and *tried really hard*. The most helpful attitude you can cultivate when meditating is one of *not* trying too hard and to resist judging each moment as either good or bad – simply notice these thoughts and moments and return your focus to the breath.

Step 8: When it's time for you to bring your meditation to an end, just sit with your eyes closed (or focussed) for a few more moments and gradually bring your attention back to the chair you are sitting in and tune into your surrounding environment. Pay attention to how you are feeling, emotionally and physically, and notice any positive effects that have occurred as part of your meditation. Don't be disappointed if you're not feeling particularly calm or if your mind was very active during the session. No meditation session is wasted and each session is different. Finally, if you have achieved some calm during your meditation, try to take this feeling with you as you start your day and resist the impulse to dash off and focus on your next task unreflectingly.

Once you start practising this form of seated mindfulness on a regular basis, you will hopefully experience subtle changes in the way you think, feel and act. You will develop a heightened awareness of the way in which your mind is continually drawn away from the present moment and how stressful, negative, automatic thoughts seize your attention and affect your mood. Developing this awareness will give you a powerful tool for managing your mood as you will be more able to draw your attention away from distracting thoughts and back to the present moment. You will also reap the rewards of living life fully by being completely immersed in the present moment, whether you are engaged in a work task, enjoying a moment of tranquillity, eating or making love. Whatever pleasant, meaningful activity you engage in, it will acquire more depth through the practice of mindfulness.

Although seated meditation builds the foundation of heightened awareness and insight into your thinking and feeling processes, everything you do on a daily basis is an opportunity to practice mindfulness. When you are carrying out a routine task at work, make a commitment to engage in it by being fully absorbed in the present moment. Try to resist the tendency to let your mind wander, thinking about leisure activities you've recently experienced or would rather be engaged in. Although this is sometimes tempting, particularly if the work task is somewhat mundane, you are actually making the experience more aversive as your mind becomes conflicted with being in the here and now and yearns to be somewhere else. The mind often tries to escape from the present moment because it craves novelty (Kabat-Zinn, 1990). By becoming absorbed in each unfolding moment, you will turn even routine tasks into rich experiences and conserve mental energy because your mind is no longer engaged in a struggle between wanting to be in the past or future but needing to engage with the present. Believe it or not, even washing the dishes is used as a formal mindfulness exercise—feeling the temperature of the water and hearing it splashing, smelling the fragrance of the soap and watching the interplay of colour and light on the bubbles.

Given the pace of modern life, it's often quite challenging to maintain a focus on the present moment throughout the day, even with the best of intentions. That's why it's helpful to *check in* periodically throughout the day and anchor yourself back into the present moment. One helpful method is the *3 minute breathing space* (Segal et al., 2002). Take time out at various times in the day to simply sit up straight and tune in your *awareness* to the present moment, asking yourself, 'What am I thinking and feeling right now?'. Then *gather* yourself and place full attention on your breathing as you have learned. This will enable your mind to reconnect with the here and now. Next, *expand* your awareness to everything within your surrounding environment so that you feel grounded in the present moment. By practising this simple technique, you can gently draw your mind away from its 'default setting' of being on autopilot constantly drifting away from the present and into the future or past. Another excellent way of anchoring yourself halfway through the day is to simply go for a walk.

Walking mindfulness practice

Similar to the practice of seated mindfulness, set time aside from your hectic daily schedule (approximately 15 minutes, perhaps during lunchtime) with the *intent* of being fully present as you go for a walk. If you're worried about the work piling up, remind yourself that this small investment of time will re-energise you and enable you to cut through tasks more swiftly. If you work through your lunch break staring at a computer screen, your energy levels are guaranteed to plummet.

When we walk, we usually do so with purpose (e.g. getting to work, going to the shops) and because these activities are routine and often mundane our minds wander and we become wrapped up in thoughts. Sometimes this process can be quite useful as walking can facilitate creative thinking or problem solving, particularly when we become mentally blocked. The act of physical movement frees our thinking processes. However, we need to differentiate between this helpful and facilitative thinking-walking activity and our tendency to engage in automatic rumination and worry leading to low mood. Making this distinction will enable you to choose between reflective walking and mindful walking.

The first thing to pay attention to is the subtle physical activities involved in the act of walking. Notice the various sensations that come into play as you transfer your weight from one foot to the other and the feeling of individual muscles engaged in your legs, body and arms as they move to the rhythm of each step. As you become immersed in this rhythm, focus on your breathing and use this as an anchor to gently draw you back to the present moment as thoughts begin to drift into your awareness. Now bring your individual senses into play to fully immerse yourself in the experience. Notice what you can see, hear, feel, smell and even taste. If your mind is particularly active, you may find the following technique helpful in drawing your attention back to the present moment while walking. It's called *5-4-3-2-1*. Focus alternately on:

- Five things you can see
- Four things you can hear
- Three things you can feel
- Two things you can smell
- One thing you can taste

As you approach the end of your walk and return to work, try to carry with you any feelings of calm that have accumulated. Even if your mind was turbulent during the walk and you found it difficult to stay in the present moment, don't be despondent. As with seated mindfulness, patience and practice will be rewarded and no session is wasted. Engaging in daily meditation is similar to Professor Seligman's notion of *psychological capital* that we encountered in Chapter 3 (Seligman, 2002). Each time you meditate or engage in a meditative practice such as mindful walking, you make a deposit in the account for your mental well-being and the benefits accrue gradually over time. Now try to think of the various ways that you can practice mindfulness in your daily life.

If you forget everything else I've taught you in this chapter, remember this:

1   Think of your body as a barometer to your overall well-being. If minor ailments persist, consider what your body is trying to tell you.

2   Use the questions on depression and anxiety as a mental health checklist. If the symptoms have lasted for more than a fortnight and occur most days, get help.

3   Inoculate yourself against stress through a combination of physical fitness, work-life balance, connection with others and personal development.

4   Mindfulness teaches us to focus on the present moment so that we get respite from brooding about the past and worrying about the future.

5   Try to practice seated mindfulness every day. The benefits are cumulative and your investment of time will be repaid in dividends through improved mental and physical well-being.

6   Use the 5-4-3-2-1 technique to practice mindful walking.

References

Baumeister, R.F. and Tierney, J. (2011). *'Willpower': rediscovering our greatest strength*. Allen Lane.

Covey, S. (1999). *The 7 habits of highly effective people*. Simon Schuster.

Csikszentmihalyi, M. (2002) *Flow: the psychology of optimal experience*. Harper Perennial.

EFSA (2010). Scientific Opinion on Dietary Reference Values for Water. *European Food Safety Authority Journal* 8(3): 1459.

Isaacson, W. (2011). *Steve Jobs: the exclusive biography*. Simon Schuster.

Kabat-Zinn, J. (1990). *Full catastrophe living*. Piatkus.

Kroenke, K., Spitzer, R.L., Williams, J.B. (2001). The PHQ9: Validity of a brief depression severity measure. *Journal of General Internal Medicine* 16(9): 606–13.

Lutz, A., L.L. Greischar, N.B. Rawlings, M. Ricard, and R.J. Davidson (2004). Long-term meditators self-induce high-amplitude gamma synchrony during mental practice. *Proceedings of the National Academy of Sciences* 101: 16369–73.

National Health Service (NHS). (2014). www.NHS.uk/livewell

Raichle, M.E., A.M. Macleod, A.Z. Snyder, W.J. Powers, D.A. Gusnard, and G.L. Shulman. (2001). A default mode of brain function. *Proceedings of the National Academy of Sciences* 98:676–682.

Segal, Z.V., Williams, J.M.G., and Teasdale, J.D. (2002). *Mindfulness-based cognitive therapy for depression*. Guilford Press.

Seligman, M.E.P. (2002). *Authentic happiness*. Free Press.

Sisson, M. (2012). *The primal blueprint*. Vermilion.

Spitzer, R.L., Kroenke, K., Williams, J.B., and Löwe, B. (2006). A brief measure for assessing generalized anxiety disorder: the GAD-7. *Archives of Internal Medicine* 166 (10): 1092–7.

Appendices for this book are available at
https://www.routledge.com/products/9781138838017

Index